Israeli Half-tracks
Volume One

including Sandwich Trucks and Armoured Cars

Tom Gannon

Text copyright © 2008 Tom Gannon

Published by Barbarossa Books
Zhukov House
14 Maldon Road
Tiptree
Essex CO5 0LL
England

British Library Cataloguing in Publication Data
Gannon, Tom
Israeli Half-track: Volume 1

ISBN 978-1-84768-001-3

Designed and produced by AMR Design Ltd (www.amrdesign.com)

All unaccredited photographs are from the Tom Gannon Collection

Every effort has been made to contact copyright holders of any material reproduced in this book. Any omissions will be rectified in subsequent printings if notice is given to the Publisher.

Barbarossa Books welcome authors who would like to submit material for possible future publication.

*The publisher is immensely grateful to
Mr Trevor Davenport, without whose input this work
would not have been possible. Thank you, my Lord.*

Russell Hadler, Proprietor

Telephone: 01621 810810
e-mail: sales@barbarossabooks.eu
website: www.barbarossabooks.eu

14 Maldon Road
Tiptree
Essex CO5 0LL
United Kingdom

Barbarossa Books

Contents

Introduction

About halfway between Tel Aviv on the coast and Jerusalem in the mountains, at a place called Latrun, there is an old fortress-like building. It sits on top of a small hill and is visible from Highway 1, partly because of the hill, but mostly due to a large number of flags and a high concrete tower topped by a Sherman tank. Today, it is the home of the Israeli Defence Force Armoured Corps Memorial and Museum, *Yad-Lshiryon* (literally, Hand to Armour). As visitors pass through the gate, past the souvenir shop, the first things they see are some of the well over 120 vehicles on display. These tanks and other armoured vehicles from Israel's past and present circle around the old fort, almost in a defensive perimeter seemingly guarding a rather subdued memorial to the thousands of Armoured Corps soldiers who have died since Israel declared its independence on 15th May 1948. Reminiscent of the Vietnam War Memorial in Washington DC, the names of the dead are inscribed on a long white plaque. The building still bears signs of battle damage sustained back in 1948-1949 when it was a former British police station manned by members of the Transjordanian Arab Legion.

The fort was a key element in the War of Independence, and even before. It guarded the road over which convoys had to travel in order to bring supplies to the Jews living in Jerusalem, who were surrounded by, at the time, hostile Arabs. These convoys were constantly under attack, which forced the *Haganah*, the predecessor to the IDF, to develop makeshift armoured vehicles to escort the supply trucks. Wrecks of these vehicles can still be seen along the road, although the road itself was moved in places, and the wrecks along with it, after Israel finally captured Latrun in 1967. The skills learned in building these "sandwich" trucks, as they were called, were put to further

The ex-British and Jordanian police station at Latrun is now the site of the Israeli Armoured Corps Memorial and Museum. Every effort has been made to preserve the building exterior as it was when the IDF finally captured it in 1967. Battle damage is covered with plexiglass in areas where a weather seal is necessary. The interior contains offices, museum exhibits and a library. Along one exterior wall, in this 1992 picture, is a memorial listing the names of the Armoured Corps members killed since 1948. The wall has since been moved away from the building to a position to the right of its location in this photograph.

use as the first truly armoured military vehicles began to arrive just prior to the outbreak of the war. Among these vehicles were the first armoured cars and half-tracks that were to sustain the IDF, along with the Sherman tank, for years to come.

This book is meant to be, primarily, a modeller's guide to the plethora of armoured vehicles used by the early IDF. The concentration is, of course, on the American-built half-tracks used in various guises from 1948 to the present. That story is best understood when considered along with the other often makeshift and hodge-podge collection of other armoured vehicles that fought alongside or in support of these half-tracks. Undoubtedly, due to the relative lack of accessible information, material has been left out. Some of the in-service photographs, particularly a few of the earlier ones, may be grainy or otherwise of poor quality. A few enlargements of small sections of photographs taken from a distance appear fuzzy, but are not too bad. They were chosen to show the variety and condition of the vehicles in use.

My usual disclaimer is that I do not claim to be an expert on this or any other subject. Instead, I am just another enthusiast who enjoys sharing what I know.

Chapter One Half-track Primer

Although not quite as complicated as the various Sherman models, there can still be some confusion about the various types of half-track; so, a brief introduction is in order.

There is a strong family resemblance to the four-wheel drive White Scout Car M3. This vehicle started life as the Scout Car M2A1, but its designation was later changed to M3. During development, it was decided to test the concept of a half-track type vehicle. One of the M2A1s was modified by White Motor Company to have a track and bogie wheel assembly replacing the rear wheels. The appearance of the Scout Car was unchanged except for the installation of the track and bogie wheel assembly. After initial testing during 1938 failed to adequately prove the concept, the vehicle was re-converted back to its original form and returned to service.

Subsequent demands from the United States Army, following the outbreak of the Second World War in 1939, prompted the construction of a new pilot vehicle. Again, this was based on the Scout Car M3. Designated the T14, this vehicle was built by White Motor Company in Cleveland, Ohio and driven to Aberdeen Proving Ground in Maryland. After further testing and modification, it was standardised in 1940 as the Half-track Car M2. Its use was intended as a scout vehicle and a prime mover for artillery.

At the same time, Diamond T Motor Car Company produced a similar conversion, designated T8, with a rear body that was ten inches longer than that of the M2, to accommodate additional troop seating. The actual wheel-base was the same, with all of the added length to the rear of the tracks. After testing, the T8 was standardised as the Half-track Personnel Carrier M3.

Another T14 test vehicle was modified to carry an 81 mm mortar firing to the rear, and standardized first as the 81 mm Mortar Carrier M4. This vehicle was designed to be primarily a transport for the mortar and crew, with onboard firing only in an emergency. However, the troops called for a vehicle that would allow routine use of the weapon from within the vehicle. With a strengthened mount, this new version was designated the M4A1.

Full-scale production was undertaken at White Motor Company for the M2/M4/M4A1 and at Diamond T Motor Car Company for the M3. When demand for half-tracks exceeded capacity, Autocar Company joined the manufacturing group, producing both M2 and M3 style vehicles. Regardless of manufacturer, the White 160AX engine powered all of these half-tracks.

The Half-track Car M2 and its related vehicles are easily distinguishable by the rear hull stopping even with the tracks, with a short step-like extension beyond them. It has no rear door. There is a track or rail around the interior to allow the crew to traverse several machine guns, generally meant to include one .50 calibre and two .30 calibre machine guns. Immediately behind the driver and co-driver positions are storage lockers that open to the outside and from above. The exterior doors, with their large latches, are very evident and serve to further identify the type. The M4 and the later M4A1 mortar carriers are essentially the same, except for the mortar and ammunition storage, of course. The mortar carriers were also fitted with rear doors.

The Personnel Carrier M3 crew compartment is ten inches longer, extending beyond the tracks to a point even with the rear of the step on the M2, and it has a rear door. Instead of the gun rail, the M3 has a pedestal mount for a .30 calibre machine gun, just behind the commander's seat, which is between the driver and co-driver. Troops often replaced the .30 calibre with a .50 calibre for more firepower.

As mentioned, the M2 was intended for use as a command, scout or towing vehicle, while the M3 was initially meant to be a personnel carrier only. However, both types were often used for other purposes, with the M3 being particularly adaptable for everything from an ambulance to self-propelled artillery. Specifications called for either vehicle to be equipped with a front-mounted unditching roller on the early vehicles, or a choice on later vehicles between the roller and a five ton-capacity winch mounted in front of the front bumper.

As production requirements increased to meet expanding war needs, it was soon obvious that further manufacturing capacity was needed, so International Harvester was asked to come in. There are significant and often very visible differences between the IHC versions and the M2/M3. First, the IHC Model RED-450-B six-cylinder engine replaced the White engine. The armour was homogeneous plate, not face-hardened, and it was welded instead of bolted together. The rear corners were rounded, and the front mudguards were flat-sectioned instead of the commercial automotive style featured on the M2/M3. Again, two types were standardised, with the M9 corresponding to the M2 and the M5 to the M3. However, both were the same length, and each had a rear door. Only internal stowage and layout distinguished the two. The M9 did not have the external side doors. Except for US training purposes, all IHC vehicles were allocated to Lend-Lease.

Further modifications were made during the production runs that resulted in different looks. The most significant of these was the deletion of the gun rail in the M2 and the machine gun pedestals in the others. A pulpit-like armoured enclosure was installed over the co-driver's position. Inside this there was a round skate rail, or ring mount, fitted with a .50 calibre machine gun. This change resulted in new designations of M2A1, M3A1, M5A1 and M9A1, respectively. The M4 and M4A1 were not modified in this fashion. The introduction of the ring mount preceded production of the M9, so that particular model never actually existed. When vehicles are identified as M9 in other references, and there is no pulpit, they are definitely M5s. In some contemporary and historical sources, production numbers for the M9 are quoted, in error. However, in reality, these are M9A1s. It was common practice to retro-fit the ring mount to earlier vehicles during overhauls and when re-building training vehicles for shipment overseas.

Mine racks were added to the sides of each production model, with those on the M2, M4/M4A1 and M2A1 beginning behind the side doors. These were also later added to earlier production vehicles. Carrying explosives on the outside of the armour was not logical to most crews, who then used the racks for other stowage instead. The headlights on the White/Diamond T vehicles were moved from the mudguards to the sides of the radiator armour. There were variations in the style of light guards between the M2/M3 and the IHC versions. Many older vehicles were also upgraded in the field, sometimes confusing the identification issue. Post-war, even more changes were made that further altered the appearance of the vehicles.

As mentioned previously, the M3 - with its longer hull - lent itself to experimentation with various types of weapons. Major self-propelled gun versions of the US half-track series included:

M3 75 mm GMC (Gun Motor Carriage) Anti-Tank Gun. The US Army used this vehicle in the Philippines in 1942, in North Africa and in Sicily. The US Marines used them as the SPM (Self-Propelled Mount). (At least one Marine SPM was based on a M2). The British issued them to the heavy gun troops of armoured car units in Italy.

T19 105 mm HMC (Howitzer Motor Carriage). The US Army in North Africa, Sicily and Italy used this on a limited basis.

T30 75 mm HMC. The US Army used this type, mounting the 75 mm pack howitzer, in limited numbers, as above.

M4, M4A1 81 mm MMC (Mortar Motor Carriage). Based on the M2, with mortar firing to the rear. Originally, the mortar was used primarily as a ground mount. However, due to demands from the field, the chassis was strengthened in the M4A1, which enabled the mortar to be fired from within the vehicle on a regular basis. Some vehicles were modified in the field to fire forward. Experiments were done using 120 mm mortars, but the chassis was found to be too light to absorb the recoil. (This was not solved until the Israelis found a way years later).

M21 MMC. This vehicle was based on the M3, with the mortar designed to fire forward from the beginning. It was built in only limited numbers, and is easily identified by its rear-mounted machine gun pedestal and the ladders on the side. Available photographic evidence of its use in combat is limited. One photograph, claiming to show a M3 in the Pacific, is actually an M21.

M13 MGMC (Machine Gun Motor Carriage) (M14 on IHC version). Built by White, this M3-based vehicle is fitted with twin .50 calibre anti-aircraft guns on an electrically powered Maxson turret M33. The British and Commonwealth nations received most of the M14s. However, they removed the guns and turrets, and used them as personnel carriers. A few were used by American units, with some being upgraded to M16 standards.

M16 MGMC (M17 on IHC version). This vehicle was modified after requests for more firepower, with four guns on the multiple .50 calibre machine gun mount M45. The Soviets used numbers of the M17. The M16 was so much in demand after the Normandy battles that an expedient type, unofficially designated M16B, was developed for conversion in the field, using standard M2 and M3 series vehicles and removing the turret from the towed version.

T28E1 M15 and M15A1 CGMC (Combination Gun Motor Carriage). This very successful vehicle was fitted with a single 37 mm cannon and two .50 calibre machine guns. The T28E1 was a non-standardised weapons system using water-cooled machine guns. It was used in small numbers from North Africa to Southern France. The M15 and M15A1 used the more common air-cooled .50 calibre M2 HB (HB = heavy barrel). The M15A1 is visually differentiated from the M15, by having the 37 mm gun mounted above the machine guns.

T48 GMC with 57 mm Anti-Tank Gun. This gun was the American-produced version of the British 6-pounder. These vehicles were issued to the British and the Soviets, although only the latter used it in combat. The British converted them back to troop carriers. These vehicles, along with the back-dated M13s, were the only White versions used by the British during the Second World War.

M3A2 (M5A2). This was the designation for the ultimate half-track, meant to replace the M2 and M3 series with a single vehicle. It featured a lengthened pulpit and ladders on the sides, as major distinguishing external features. It did not enter production beyond the prototypes. Some features, such as the ladders, were, however, added to existing vehicles over time.

There were also numerous experimental vehicles, most of which were never accepted for troop use. Some M15s in the Pacific Theatre were later modified with 40 mm guns replacing the combination gun mount. These M15 "Specials" were used in the Philippines and again later in Korea.

This fully restored M3 Scout Car is part of the collection at the Virginia Museum of Military Vehicles in Nokesville, Virginia. There is more than a superficial resemblance between the Scout Car and its descendant, the Half-track Car M2. From the front, they are indistinguishable, although differences quickly become apparent beyond the windscreen.

It is from the rear that the differences become obvious. Even so, there is still a family resemblance, particularly since the lack of a rear door was carried forward to the M2. This seemingly illogical approach was later remedied with the Personnel Carrier M3 and the Mortar Motor Carriage M4, but the design of the M2 was never changed. The flaw was finally corrected in Israeli service.

A second, totally unrestored, example is also located at the Virginia Museum of Military Vehicles. It offers a good view of the empty engine bay, and shows just how extensive restorations like that in the previous photographs can be. Compare this to the IDF vehicles being serviced in 1948, shown later.

The next few photographs show the restoration in progress. This is the instrument panel in the partially restored interior. Note the individually powered windshield wipers and the method for mounting the panes of glass for the windscreen.

This is a good view of the rear of the radiator and the guard for the fan. There are other views of the radiator and engine bay elsewhere in this book.

Compare this view to the previous photograph of the unrestored Scout Car.

This is the engine bay of a rather sad-looking unrestored half-track in West Virginia. This is very similar in layout to that in the Scout Car. Look at the attention to detail in the restored vehicle.

This photograph clearly shows how the bonnet (hood) operates. Photographs of the later upgraded IDF vehicles show that, in addition to the existing side-opening hinges, the Israelis added another rear hinge to allow the bonnet to open from the front. The headlight guard marks the original location for the automotive style headlights that were also used on the half-track as well.

The Half-track Car M2 was later upgraded to the standard shown here. This Half-track Car M2A1 is on display in Tel Aviv, Israel, but it is totally unmodified from its form as acquired by the Israelis. Actually, this vehicle appears to be a straight M2 that was upgraded to M2A1 standards, with the substitution of the M49 Ring Mount for the original interior skate rail. The automotive style headlight is more indicative of the M2. *(David Levy)*

The mine racks and the pulpit are standard for the M2A1. However, the groups of four bolts in a row indicate where the skate rail was attached. Production M2A1s would not have these. *(David Levy)*

This is the characteristic step at the rear of the track run. Note also the lack of a rear door, common to the M2 and M2A1. *(David Levy)*

The mounting points for the skate rail are again evident in this view. The left side bin opens at the top and to the outside. Crew seating is limited in the M2. The rails between the bins are for the commander's seat back, facing forward, and a crewman's seat facing to the rear. *(David Levy)*

This view forward shows the ring mount to advantage. Note that the right side bin does not open to the top. Although not evident here, a radio was often mounted to the top. *(David Levy)*

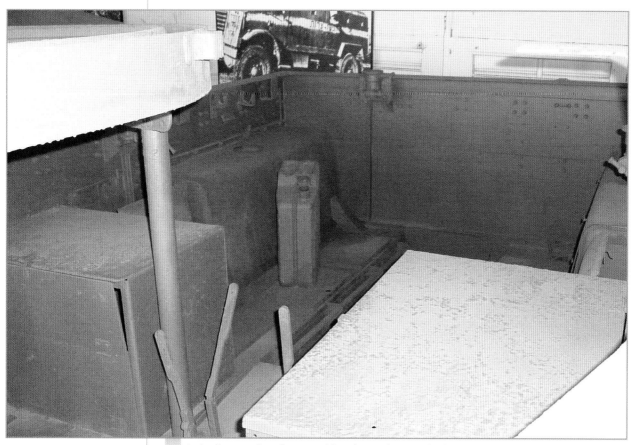

The lack of a rear door is very evident here. The crew had to disembark over the sides, with the obvious disadvantages. Most Israeli vehicles were modified to eliminate this problem. *(David Levy)*

The World War Two Vehicle Museum in Hubbard, Ohio is home to this expertly restored, and rare, Mortar Motor Carriage M4A1. Noticeable features are the internal skate rail, the later style headlights and the short mine rack.

This close-up of the left side shows the back side of the skate rail and the external door to the interior storage bin. The mine rack even contains some (hopefully) dummy mines.

The rear door is seen here, as are additional storage bins. There are also reinforced supports under the bins, which also function as steps for the crew to use when firing the mortar.

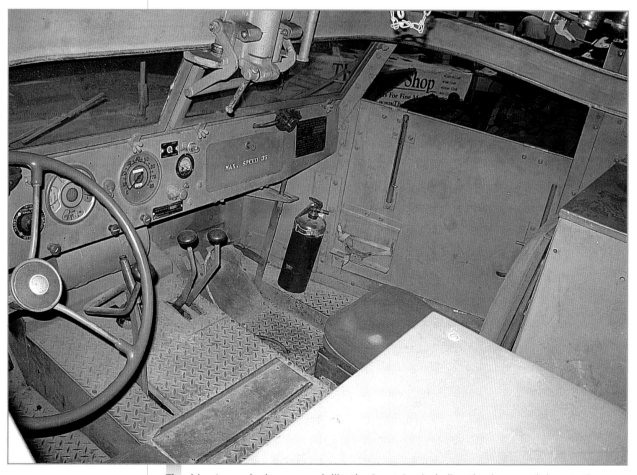

The driver's area looks very much like the Scout Car, including the downward slope to the skate rail. Part of the machine gun mount is visible.

The left side box and ammunition storage are shown here. Mortar bombs were carried in protective tubes. The skate rail on the M2 would look just like this one. In this case, both bins open from the top, as well as externally.

The right side is almost a mirror image of the left, except for a couple of fittings. Unlike with the original M4, the mortar in the M4A1 is meant to be fired regularly from onboard, thus the reinforced base. Crew seating is much like the M2/M2A1.

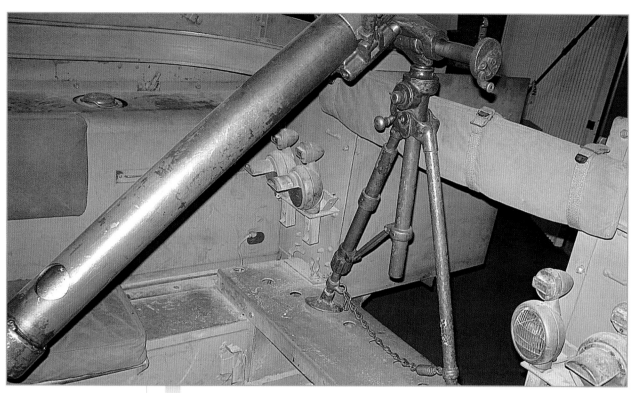

This is a nice detail view of the rear interior. The mortar was traversed by moving the legs to different holes. A wider arc required turning the vehicle. Beneath the plate is stowage for boxes of machine gun ammunition. Other points of interest include the spare lights, the mortar bomb on the floor and the storage clip for a rifle along the side below the seat cushions. Although there is a rear door, getting in and out was a little difficult, thus the cushion wrap on the skate rail.

As with the M2, the M3 was also often upgraded to this configuration, resulting in a mix of features that adds confusion regarding the original designation as built. This beautifully restored half-track, belonging to the VMMV, looks like a production M3A1, however. Note the location of the armoured pulpit for the ring-mounted machine gun, relative to the windscreen. Many Israeli vehicles began life with a ring mount, but these were removed during the various IDF upgrades.

The rear stowage racks commonly seen on many half-tracks were not actually standardised as an original factory item until the M3A2. (This view is ideal for backdating the Tamiya M3A2. All of the external changes/deletions can be determined here).

This view of the passenger side shows several distinguishing features of the White/Diamond T vehicles. The commercial truck mudguards, headlights and armoured door flap are unique to these half-tracks. Compare the smooth inside face of the door flap with the International Harvester version shown later. The crossed sabre plate is not a factory item.

Photographs of vehicles that are in less than good condition, offer the opportunity to see features that are otherwise concealed. This photograph, taken at Aberdeen Proving Ground, may be used, along with several others in the main part of the book, to model the battery compartment in detail.

This International Harvester vehicle is on display at the French armour museum at Saumur, France. The armoured visor on the door is located on the inside face, while the ones on the White/Diamond T versions are on the outside. Note the flat mudguards and different style of headlight guard. Also, note the lack of bolts on the troop compartment armour, and the sliding visor on the inside of the door.

Other distinguishing features of the IHC versions include rounded rear corners and a rear bumper style common to American commercial lorries. All IHC half-tracks came with a rear door, regardless of purpose. As with the White vehicles, the rear stowage racks are later additions. This vehicle is on display in Israel, and is featured in more detail later. The upper tail-lights are an Israeli addition.

This M3A1 is part of the World War Two Vehicle Museum. Note the wiring for the headlight, which is itself mounted to the side of the vehicle, rather than on the mudguard. Note also the bracing in the wheel well.

This vehicle has a non-standard installation for a radio. Otherwise, it is a standard production M3A1.

The interior right side looks very standard. This offers a good view of the machine gun installation. This museum was the site for AMPS 2006, a show for armour model builders, which explains the vendor table visible over the side and through the door.

This is an excellent view of the inside of the pulpit, with skate rail and machine gun mounting.

This is the interior of the VMMV M3A1. The seats folded forward, as shown here. Note the map holder in the door and the bracket for a fire-extinguisher on the bulkhead.

This is the standard interior layout for the M3A1. The angled post on the left is for a radio antenna, while the horizontal rod is one of the supports for a tarpaulin. (Compare this layout to that of the M2A1 in Tel Aviv-Jaffa).

This rear view of the same M3A1 shows two of the three machine gun pintle mounts, as well as a rifle rack behind the seat. A hinge for the lower-seat locker is just visible behind the three-seat cushion from the rear.

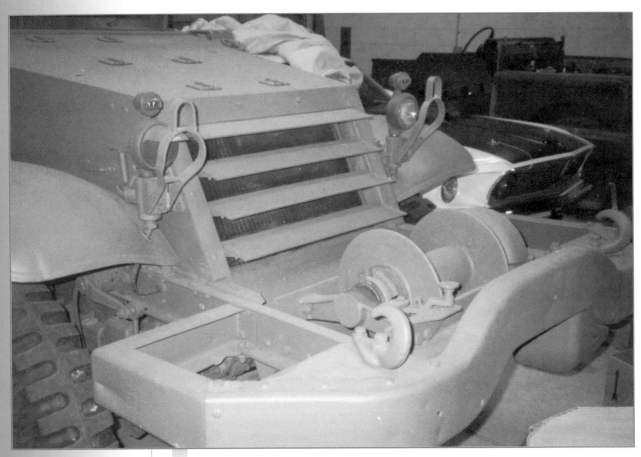

This is a good view of the front winch, without the cable itself, as well as the redesigned headlights and brush guards.

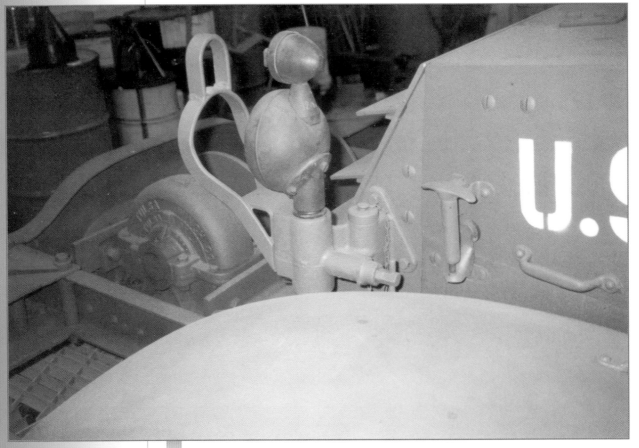

This close-up view shows the unique shape of the light guard. It also shows the bonnet latch and lifting handle. Note the bolt heads.

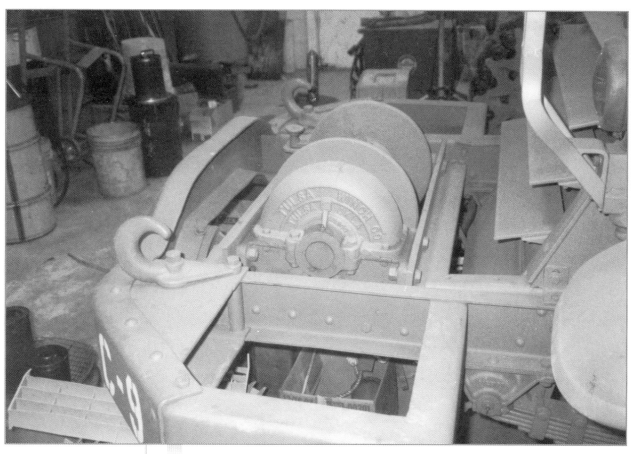

Here is a clear view of the left side of the winch. Note the casting marks with the name "TULSA WINCH CO." at the top and "TULSA OKLA" below that. Unlike the rest of the vehicle, the bumper is riveted, rather than bolted, together.

This is a rare view of the bumper, without the winch installed. The US Army Ordnance Museum at Aberdeen Proving Ground, Maryland, is actively restoring the vehicles in its collection, as it is able to do so. This vehicle has not yet made it to the programme, unfortunately.

The suspension unit included one bogie unit per side, each with eight wheels with rubber tyres and one double steel return roller. The volute springs are smaller versions of those used on the Sherman tank. The drive sprocket is at the front, with an idler at the rear.

The exhaust pipe comes out on the right side, between the sprocket and the bogie unit. The tracks are rubber, over a steel web.

This chassis awaits restoration at Mil-Spec Restorations, a workshop in New Jersey that specialises in military vehicles. It is an IHC vehicle with the flat mudguards, not shown here. The condition of the vehicle, one of two here, offers the opportunity to see areas not normally visible.

This is the idler wheel. Note also the heavy spring for the rear tow hook.

The final drive and drive sprocket unit sits about thirty metres away, under a tree.

There is some variation between units. The bogie truck in the previous photograph is plain, while this one has casting marks. This is the rear face.

The front face is a little simpler. Note the large coil spring to the rear on each side of the vehicle.

There is an excellent private collection of softskin vehicles in West Virginia, know as Top Kick's Museum. Among the many Jeeps and American-built lorries is this old Machine Gun Motor Carriage M16. It is actually the first vehicle to catch a visitor's eye. Recovered from a construction project, it awaits restoration. The object sitting in it is an aircraft drop tank fashioned to resemble a rocket launcher. It is presented here as an example of the fate that awaited many surplus armoured vehicles. Little remains to identify its original function, but it offers an interesting comparison to the M16 at Aberdeen, Maryland.

This M16 MGMC is on display next to the museum building at Aberdeen Proving Ground. It has seen better days, but it serves to show the overall layout of the vehicle type. Compare it to the Israeli modified vehicles. Although it is a true M16, as indicated by the shape of the folding armour, the gun mount seen here is actually a ground mount just sitting inside.

This rear view shows the folding armour, designed to allow full traverse, and maximum depression, for the guns. However, be careful when using museum vehicles for reference: some vehicles at APG are test platforms, with unusual fittings. This one, though, simply has a ground mount gun turret dropped into place to replace its missing original assembly.

The M45 mount for the quad 50s on the M16 and M17 is a compact affair, allowing for 360 degree traverse. Elevation is within the range of -10 degrees to +90 degrees. The gunner sits behind a circular shield. This bare unit is in one of the storage sheds at Saumur.

This M16 at the VMMV is still under restoration. Without the guns, this view shows the basic attachment points for them and the ammunition cans. Note the gearing for the elevation mechanism.

The completed M16 is shown here. With the wiring and generator in place, the mount is a little more complex. The U-shaped bracket supports a small platform for the two loaders. With this fitted, the Maxson turret was designated M45D.

The folding armour is shown here. On the M13, the plates were straight. The additional guns on the M16 required a cutout, as shown. The unofficial M16B did not have the folding armour, resulting in a much higher profile, similar to the Israeli TCM20.

This M15A1 is displayed at the post museum at Fort Lewis, Washington State. The vehicle display was off limits on this particular day, so the photographs were a little rushed. This vehicle is equipped with the front roller, instead of the winch.

The armour around the gun itself was added after combat experience with the T28E1. Examples of this vehicle are rare. The triangular fitting behind the driver compartment prevents the gun from hitting its own vehicle. There is a M3A1 in the background.

Israeli Half-tracks and Early Armoured Vehicles

From the time of the Diaspora, there had always been a small, generally religious, Jewish population in Palestine. Through to the end of the 19th Century, these people were concentrated around the larger cities. With the advent of Zionism – the philosophy of the return of Jews to the ancient homeland of Israel – European Jews began to emigrate in increasing numbers. A discussion of the relative merits and causes of Zionism is best left to others. However, the resultant influx of people with aspirations for a Jewish state was bound to be a source of conflict with a variety of groups, most of whom arrived in the area from elsewhere as well.

The new immigrants established settlements that were primarily agricultural in nature. With these settlements scattered throughout the territory, there was friction with the local Arabs, themselves descendants of a much earlier wave of immigration following the Muslim conquest of Palestine. That part of history, too, is a subject best left to others. It was during this initial phase of increasingly violent conflict that the first organised Jewish defence organisation, Hashomer, was created. These "watchmen" guarded the new settlements and created a model for future organisations. As soon as technology allowed, this model included the use of improvised armoured vehicles. Used mostly along the roads between *kibbutzim* (agricultural settlements) and other Jewish enclaves, to protect supply convoys from Arab attacks, they provided a basis for a developing industrial capacity.

The First World War was the backdrop for a rise in Arab nationalism to go along with its Jewish counterpart. Jews fought for both the British on the Allied side and for Turkey on the Central Powers' side during the war, each group hoping for supportive benefactors after the war. It did not work out that way, but the war did provide basic combat training for the people who were to be the leaders of the future Israeli Army.

Any post-war sense of security resulting from the British Mandate soon evaporated. The violence quickly escalated, culminating in the 1920 Passover riots. The perception among the Jewish population that the British were either apathetic or even partial to the Arabs, resulted in the creation of the *Hagana*, which is the official forerunner of the Israeli Defence Force (IDF).

For the next sixteen years, tensions increased as the Jewish population increased. This tension was fuelled by the escalating anti-Semitic violence in Europe and, later on, by the pro-Nazi sympathies of the Grand Mufti of Jerusalem. Bloody rioting in 1929 and 1936 resulted in the Jews taking more and more direct responsibility for the defence of the far-flung kibbutzim as well as for the supply convoys travelling in between.

A sympathetic British officer, Captain Orde Wingate, convinced the British Army to allow the formation of a Jewish fighting unit known as the Special Night Squads. This force defended the settlements and even conducted raids of its own against Arab militants until the *Hagana* became active after the Second World War. The Squads made use of a motley collection of homemade armoured vehicles built around mostly civilian cars and lorries. Some of these were actually quite crude, if not downright comical looking. They served a purpose, and, more importantly, they provided much needed experience for the people who would eventually work on more useful vehicles later on.

With the dramatic increase in illegal Jewish immigration after the Second World War, the need for armed defence increased also. The *Palmach*, the military arm of the *Hagana*, provided armed escorts, *Meshuryanim* ("armoured cars"), for the supply convoys travelling the roads. Lacking an adequate supply of proper armour plate, and using experience gained with the very crude vehicles used before the war, the Jewish engineers developed makeshift armour plating consisting of wood sandwiched between two metal sheets. Sometimes other materials, such as concrete and sand, were used as the filler for what became known as "Sandwich Trucks". Regardless of the material, the weight gain and loss of performance and carrying capacity was considerable, but the amount of protection was more than adequate against the weapons available to the Arab militias.

The "Battle for the Roads" continued up to and during the War of Independence. A popular Arab tactic was to build a roadblock to stop the escorted convoys long enough to allow a concentrated attack on the exposed vehicles. To combat this, some of the sandwich trucks were fitted with battering rams. These were simple affairs consisting of a triangular metal frame, usually hinged and attached to the front bumper. When lowered, the typical ram rested on a skid that slid along the surface, preventing it from digging into the ground. One of these ram-equipped makeshift armoured lorries, with the nickname "Monster", is displayed at The Collection Houses museum in Tel Aviv-Jaffa.

The first lorry conversions were basically personnel carriers with firing slits in the sides. Various types of lorry were used, including civilian models. The more commonly used vehicles seemed to be Canadian-built CMP patterns, along with US $1\frac{1}{2}$ and $2\frac{1}{2}$ ton Dodge and GMC models. The work was done to standardised designs, but by a number of workshops, resulting in some minor differences between them. Some were equipped with upwardly swinging hatches in the roof, sometimes referred to as "butterflies", from which crewmen could also fire light weapons. Other lorries were open-topped affairs. Two examples of these makeshift armoured fighting vehicles are preserved at the IDF Collection Houses museum in Tel Aviv, although one of them is a recovered battlefield wreck. There are also two well-done mock-up sandwich trucks on display, at Latrun and at the Givati Brigade museum. Supply lorries also sometimes had armoured cabs to protect the drivers, but they were otherwise dependent on the escorts.

At first, the Arab forces were mostly local militias, joined later by a more formally trained National Guard. Although ambush was a common tactic, some of the actions were pitched battles between battalion-sized units. Later, following the declaration of the State of Israel, the young IDF had to face the combined armies of Egypt, Syria, Trans-Jordan, Lebanon and Iraq. It was then that they needed more than these simple lightly armoured lorries.

By 1947, as plans were finalised for a declaration of statehood and full-scale war approached, these improvised fighting vehicles evolved into true armoured cars, some with and some without machine gun turrets. Again, two generally standardised types of fully-enclosed vehicles were used, along with open-topped personnel carriers and supply vehicles. As they did with the earlier sandwich trucks, technicians used a variety of vehicles. Since different shops did the work, there were some differences between vehicles, even when a standard chassis like the Dodge $\frac{3}{4}$ ton Weapons Carrier was used. The armour was still the sandwich wood/metal type.

One enclosed design was essentially a primitive infantry-fighting vehicle with firing slits along the sides and rear. The other was a true armoured car with the same type of firing slit, plus a front-mounted machine gun and a machine gun turret. Multiple designs, based on a number of base vehicles, were built. The turreted models were limited to the $\frac{3}{4}$ ton or 15 cwt classes, while personnel carriers were built on this size vehicle as well as the larger $2\frac{1}{2}$ to 3-ton class. Armoured flaps protected the radiator in a manner similar to the American half-track and M3 Scout Car. In another of the ironies of weapons use in the IDF, the machine gun of choice for many years was the Czech version of the German MG 34. When American trucks with left-hand drive were used, the front mounted machine guns, with some in ball mounts, were on the right side. When British vehicles with right-hand drive were used, the guns were on the left. The photograph section of this book shows a variety of vehicle types and body styles. In addition to the few surviving vehicles in Tel Aviv, there are a number of derelicts along the main motorway between Tel Aviv and Jerusalem. These are mostly just the armoured bodies, plus a few frames. One of them is what remains of a wrecker. Some are obviously of the same design, perhaps built in the workshop, as the museum exhibits.

Existing armoured vehicles, like the American M3 Scout Car and some British armoured cars, such as at least one Otter Mk I, were also converted to include turret-mounted machine guns. The turrets on all of these makeshift armoured cars were generally built to a standard design, although there were some detail differences, such as forward or side opening hatches. There were some minor differences in size on some of them as well. Real armour plate was still scarce, so the sandwich variety of the older vehicles continued in use. Turrets, however, appear to be all-metal, without regard to the base vehicle. Unfortunately, the only surviving evidence of the converted M3 Scout Car is a rusted and very sad-looking body shell at Radar Hill (*Har Adar*) near Jerusalem. (Perhaps, we may eventually see a mock-up version using one of the many privately-owned M3 Scout Cars that exist around the world).

Since the Arab forces were equipped with little in the way of modern armour, other than some armoured cars and some obsolete pre-war tanks, these home-grown vehicles proved to be very useful. Some of them remained in service into the early 1950s.

At the same time that this manufacturing effort was taking place, other efforts were underway to obtain real armoured vehicles overseas. The successful search for some useful Sherman medium tanks is described in the author's book, *Israeli Sherman*. Although the IDF also acquired two Cromwell cruiser tanks and a few pre-Second World War French Renaults, the brunt of the fighting was done by the ad hoc collection of converted and upgraded light armoured vehicles described above, along with increasing numbers of American-built Second World War half-tracks.

The first of these half-tracks, disguised as agricultural tractors and painted red, were actually obtained in 1947, probably in the United Kingdom, and stored in a warehouse in Tel Aviv. The ruse was not actually that far-fetched, because many surplus military vehicles, including tanks and half-tracks, were finding their way into civilian use all over the world. Surplus half-tracks, in fact, were common sights with American volunteer fire departments in rural areas, and may even still be in use today. (The author had plans, at a younger age, to convert the Tamiya M3A2 into a half-tracked fire engine, based on photographs of several vehicles, taken in the 1970s. One of them had fire-fighting equipment in the rear, and was painted gloss red with typical gold fire department markings! Another had its rear armour replaced by shiny corrugated steel plates. Alas, these photographs have since disappeared).

In the early months of 1948, the British intercepted yet another shipment of fifty vehicles, as the *Hagana* tried to run the blockade. Thirty-seven of these were sent back to Britain, but they made their way back shortly after the State of Israel was declared. The other thirteen were likely left behind when the British pulled out of Palestine, and were taken over by the newly-formed Israel Defence Force. Another clandestine shipment was lost later, actually well after combat was in full swing in November 1948, when the Egyptians intercepted a ship carrying forty half-tracks.

Additional shipments arrived from various scrap and surplus dealers, mainly from Italy, which was also the source of the first Israeli Shermans. All of these early vehicles, as seen in available photographs, were International Harvester types, originally distributed as part of the Lend-Lease programme to Britain, the Commonwealth nations and France. One Israeli source identifies some of these vehicles in these early batches as being M4 mortar carriers and machine gun motor carriages formerly used by the US Fifth Army. However, this is not reflected in the photographs from the War of Independence. If they did arrive in country before the end of the war, they were not ready for service in time before hostilities ended. Photographic evidence of White/Diamond T vehicles does not appear until the 1950s.

Additionally, small numbers of Second World War armoured cars were obtained before and during the war. These included at least two ex-British Daimler Mk I armoured cars, Humber Mk IIIs captured from Egypt, a few Otter Mk Is and several Marmon-Herrington Mark IV Fs acquired from British stocks or captured from the Arab Legion. Daimler Dingo and Humber scout cars are preserved in various museums in Israel, with a number of sources stating that these also were used by the IDF. There is also film evidence of what appears to be a Humber Light Recce Car Mk I, with a small turret, in use during the 1948 war. Approximately fifty captured Universal or Bren Carriers, along with some ex-Syrian light tanks, were pressed into service as well.

During the war, being short on tanks, the young IDF modified some of its newly acquired half-tracks by adding guns of various types. Some of these had 20 mm guns and machine guns in turrets mounted over the rear crew compartment. Photographic analysis indicates that one of the turret designs allowed for 360 degree traverse, while a larger design appears to be fixed. The latter may have been one of a kind. Three vehicles were modified to mount 6-pounder anti-tank guns in a style reminiscent of the American Gun Motor Carriage M3 of Second World War fame. One of these was converted using an IHC M5 that bore markings dated November 1945, showing that it was supposed to be shipped from Montreal (Quebec) to Letterkenny Army Depot in Carlisle (Pennsylvania). The assumption is that it was intercepted somewhere in between. However, a lot of war materiel was later acquired by Israel from Canada, so it may have been a legitimate, rather than a clandestine, purchase.

The IDF practice of mounting several additional machine guns on its armoured vehicles had its origins with these modified half-tracks. The most common weapon used was the Czech post-war version of the MG 34, although Bren Guns and Besa machine guns were also used. The ubiquitous US .30 calibre came into use later.

Most half-tracks, however, were used as personnel carriers, with many having ball-mounted MG 34s added to the co-driver's position in an early attempt to create an infantry fighting vehicle. The conversion involved cutting the armoured windscreen in roughly one-third and two-third sections, and permanently bolting down the right side. These vehicles fought alongside the converted M3 Scout Cars, armoured cars and sandwich trucks during most of the major campaigns, including Operation *Horev* in December 1948.

Considering the motley collection of armour possessed by the Arab armies, the Israeli forces were surprisingly well-equipped with these makeshift but very effective fighting vehicles. The best that the Syrians presented were some obsolete French Hotchkiss and Renault tanks. They also had a few converted armoured lorries of their own. The Egyptians had Universal Carriers, some British light tanks built before the Second World War and armoured cars, including Staghounds and Humber Mk IIIs. The best-equipped and trained force was the Arab Legion of Trans-Jordan. Even its armour capabilities, however, were limited to Marmon-Herrington Mk IVF armoured cars.

Half-tracks were prominent in all of the major campaigns during the War of Independence. One of the earliest was the second of three unsuccessful assaults, Operations Ben Nun, Ben Nun II and Yoram, against the Arab Legion defending the former British police fortress at Latrun on 30th May 1948, just shortly after the establishment of the State of Israel. This attack was led by David "Mickey" Marcus, an American, who was later portrayed by Kirk Douglas in the movie *Cast a Giant Shadow*. The attacking force, from the newly organised 7th Mechanised (Armoured) Brigade, included thirteen half-tracks, possibly those left behind when the British intercepted the aforementioned shipment, and twenty converted armoured cars. The attack was repulsed, with heavy casualties both in men and equipment. Half-tracks, not armed in an earlier unsuccessful assault, but mounting machine guns at this time, actually reached the fortress, but many of them were destroyed by Arab anti-tank weapons. A third attempt on 9th June also failed. Later, the more successful Operation Danny was launched to capture the towns of Lod, Ramle, Latrun and Ramallah. The IDF briefly captured the Latrun station, but they were soon driven out by a Jordanian counter-attack. The fortress was not subdued until the Six Day War in 1967. The police station itself, still bearing signs of battle damage from 1948, is the basis for Yad-L'Shiryon, the Israeli Armoured Corps Memorial and Museum.

Marcus was also responsible for helping to build a bypass around Latrun known as the "Burma Road". This enabled a flow of supplies to reach the surrounded Jewish enclave in Jerusalem. A portion of the road still exists in the foothills near Jerusalem, above and roughly parallel to the motorway from Tel Aviv. In 1948, it was the scene of a series of skirmishes and pitched battles, as the IDF tried to keep the supply line open.

A member of the group of foreign volunteers collectively known as *Machal*, Marcus was later accidentally killed by one of his own sentries. *Machal* is a Hebrew acronym for *Mitnadvei Hutz La'Aretz*, or "Volunteers from Outside Israel". Approximately 3,500 volunteers, including non-Jews, from thirty-seven countries, fought in the Israel Defence Force during the War of Independence. Of this number, nearly five hundred were Americans or Canadians, a large number of whom served in the 7th Armoured Battalion as replacements for those lost in the Latrun attack. These volunteers helped the IDF grow from approximately thirty thousand in May 1948 to approximately ninety thousand by the end of the war in 1949.

The 79th Armoured Battalion, near the Lebanon border, was equipped with two companies of mechanised infantry in unmodified M5 half-tracks, along with two companies of armoured cars built on the Dodge ¾ ton Weapons Carrier. One of these half-tracks was driven by a young eighteen-year-old American volunteer, a Machalnik, named Ralph Lowenstein. He recalls that the heavy weapons company, perhaps just a platoon, equipped with machine guns, was composed almost entirely of very religious Jews. Many of them wore the characteristic long sideburn curls, known as earlocks, which they tucked behind their ears. They also maintained a strictly kosher diet, which required them to use half of their British mess kits for meat dishes and the other half for dairy dishes. He also described the half-track as "a wonderful instrument, except for not being covered on top by armour". Its drawback was that "it was a very vulnerable weapon in city fighting, where streets were narrow, and grenades could be dropped from rooftops".

The three 6-pounder half-tracks were used in the south, against the Egyptian armoured forces. In a single action, the commander of this unit, Hertz Hershberg, faced an attacking force of twelve M22 Locust tanks. By his personal account, his crew knocked out eight of them. A published account says that the count was five. Regardless, the attack was turned back.

By the end of the War of Independence in 1949, there were more than two hundred half-tracks in service, equipping a number of battalions. Photographs show that these vehicles were primarily International Harvester built M5s. Mixed in, as seen in photographs, were a few M14 anti-aircraft Gun Motor Carriages, with their gun turrets removed. These vehicles were supplied to both Britain and the Soviet Union via Lend-Lease during the Second World War. The Soviets used the M14, along with the more powerfully armed M17, as intended. The British, however, removed the gun turrets and used the vehicles as personnel carriers, which helps to confirm the UK as the source for theses particular vehicles.

Additional surplus half-tracks were acquired from scrap and surplus dealers in the UK, particularly at Hounslow and Newcastle, and Continental Europe where there were large surplus vehicle dumps. During the early 1950s, some were even acquired directly through the British government.

By the Sinai Campaign in 1956, known in Israel as Operation Kadesh, there were over four hundred in service. Besides the original M5s from 1948, there were now numbers of M5A1/M9A1 versions equipped with the M49 armoured ring-mounted machine gun, and various White/Diamond T models. Some of these latter vehicles may have actually been acquired during or immediately after the 1948 conflict, although there is no available photographic evidence at this point in time. The early makeshift self-propelled gun versions seem to have disappeared by this time – probably having been re-converted to troop carriers. Photographs in this book show that, during this campaign, half-tracks were in use as APCs and as prime movers for artillery, particularly 25-pounder gun/howitzers.

At this time, another type entered service: the 81 mm mortar carrier. Some of these were possibly M4/ M4A1 types or even the rare M21. However, the Israelis also mounted the mortar in other versions, like the M14 and the basic M3. Introduced in 1952, the 81 mm carrier, designated Mk C by the IDF, continued in service into the 1980s. Some of these were also given to the Lebanese Christian militias.

Horse cavalry is not a typical image for the Israeli military. At a glance, this troop could be any mounted unit from the Spanish Civil War. In actual fact, it is an IDF cavalry unit participating in a parade in April 1950. Mounted patrols were an integral part of the settlement defences from the beginning of the Arab-Jewish conflict. They continue even today in areas along the border not accessible to motor vehicles. *(David Eldan, Israeli Government Press Office)*

Members of one of the Special Night Squads are seen training in their makeshift armoured lorry at Kibbutz Maoz Haim in 1938. The armour is essentially a box built around the original lorry cab. The armoured cab is metal, while the fighting compartment may be sandwich-type armour. The crew's equipment is ex-British, including Enfield rifles and a Lewis machine gun. Building these crude armoured vehicles provided valuable experience for the future. *(Kluger Zoltan, Israeli Government Press Office)*

This rear look shows some of the ingenuity that went into the design. Egress for the crew was through an opening in the armour into the lorry bed. Assuming that the tailgate was functional, the crew could exit the vehicle without climbing over the sides. It appears to be a civilian lorry, pressed into service. *(Kluger Zoltan, Israeli Government Press Office)*

Some of the early attempts at building armoured vehicles were quite crude, if not comical looking. This one is built on a commercial automobile or a light lorry. A rudimentary turret and firing ports, along with the raised roof panels or screens preceded more sophisticated attempts, and provided much needed experience to the mechanics and engineers who would eventually become the IDF Ordnance Corps. *(Kruger Zoltan, Israeli Government Press Office)*

Just as the IDF was unable to capture Latrun in 1948, they were also unable to reach the area of Mount Scopus in Jerusalem, which included the Hebrew University and the Hadassah Hospital. This left a small enclave of Jews, including a small garrison, within the Arab section of the city. Under an agreement with Jordan, the Israelis were permitted to provide supplies and rotate the garrison and staff bi-weekly. Two armoured buses were used for this purpose. These buses are seen here preparing to leave for the trip through Jordanian territory. This routine continued until the rest of Jerusalem was captured in 1967. *(Israeli Government Press Office)*

The buses were very basic and crude conversions from commercial vehicles. They survive to this day, on display at the IDF Collection Houses in Tel Aviv-Jaffa. This museum is a very comprehensive collection of IDF artefacts, including firearms, artillery, and vehicles from all of Israel's wars, including captured equipment. It is highly recommended. (As of this writing, it appears as though this museum is due to close, with the collection to be broken up and redistributed elsewhere).

This is the smaller of the two buses. Vision was poor, and the armour was probably more of a psychological comfort factor than anything else. The armour was of the typical sandwich variety shown on the true fighting vehicles covered later. This photograph was taken in May 2005.

The vehicle has been repaired and modified for display purposes by raising the roof to provide better interior lighting. The thickness of the sandwich armour is very evident though the driver's side window.

The garrison on Mount Scopus was allowed, by treaty, to keep its small arms for defence. However, the IDF felt it would be prudent to provide additional weapons. The buses were modified with secret compartments to smuggle the weapons, as well as other so-called contraband material. In this case, the area behind the passenger seats was used.

The larger of the two buses has not been externally modified for the display. As can be seen, there was no standard to the initial conversions. Both buses are fitted with firing ports.

This is the driver's position in the larger bus. It looks like the original bus body was removed and replaced by the armoured version in roughly the same configuration. The armoured flaps over the front windows were opened or closed by a simple handle. Note the left-hand drive on both buses.

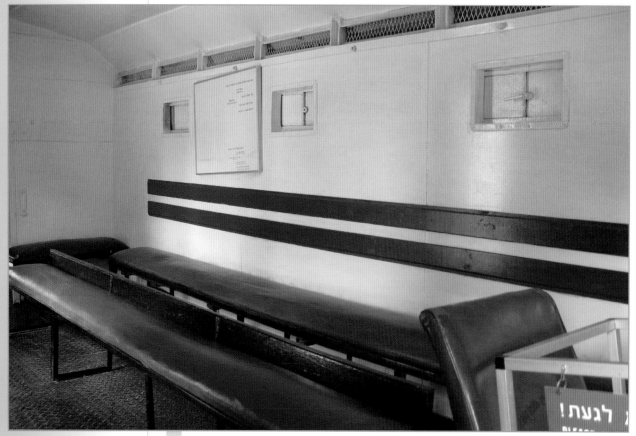

For all intents and purposes, this appears to be a simple personnel transport. Given the age of the bus, and considering the visitor traffic through the years, the seat cushions are probably replacements. Note the firing ports with sliding doors and the air vents along the bulkhead.

Behind the main passenger compartment, there is a smaller area that was used to smuggle arms. The museum staff has stocked this particular cutaway area with material typical of that hidden here. Enough arms and ammunition were brought through in this manner to allow the garrison to hold out during the 1967 fighting until it was relieved. Sources indicate that even a Jeep was disassembled, smuggled in piece by piece, and then reassembled.

By comparing the position of the firing port with the interior view, the size of this rear section can be approximated. (The curious fellow is David "Didi" Levy, a good friend of the author. Didi was "tour guide" for Josh Weingarten and the author on a recent trip to Israel. He also contributed photographs shown elsewhere in this book).

The Collection Houses contain a number of exhibits covering the entire history of the Israel Defence Force, including vehicles of the *Haganah* and *Palmach*. This is a nicely preserved "sandwich truck", of the type used to protect convoys carrying supplies to the kibbutzim. It is built on a surplus US military truck, possibly a $2\frac{1}{2}$ ton GMC.

The thickness of the sandwich armour is evident around the door window. The truck is painted a blueish grey, which may or may not be accurate. The white stripe was used, however, as required by the British to identify Jewish vehicles. This particular truck was driven in parades as recently as 1978 and perhaps later. *(David Levy)*

Points of interest in this rear three-quarter view are the hinged fender and the sliding doors on the gun apertures. Note the armour thickness. *(David Levy)*

There appear to be two jerrican racks on the rear. The "sandwich" armour plates are pre-fabricated with bolts, and then the assemblies are welded together. *(David Levy)*

The passenger seat is missing, although part of the frame remains. Note the construction of the sliding flaps on the door and the gun slit. *(David Levy)*

The armoured windscreen hatches opened and closed using a rather simple set of curved handles. Note also that the floor has some thin armour plating as well. *(David Levy)*

The spare tyre is just sitting there, so it is probably not its official location. There may also have some additional seating in the centre, upon which the crew may have stood to fire through the overhead "butterfly" screens. *(David Levy)*

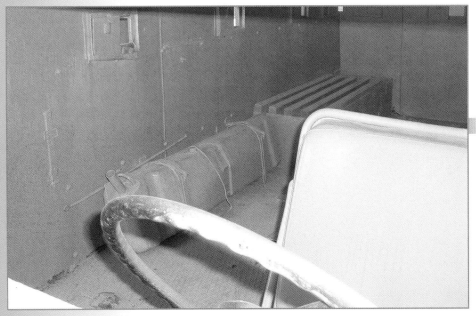

The interior is not very elaborate. In addition to a wooden seat over the wheel well, the fuel tank is crudely secured with straps. *(David Levy)*

The hatches were simple screens, more for protection from grenades or debris than anything else. A tarpaulin would be needed for weather protection. *(David Levy)*

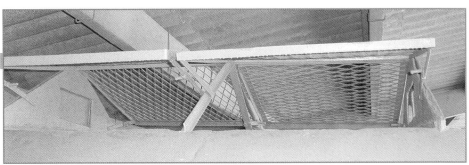

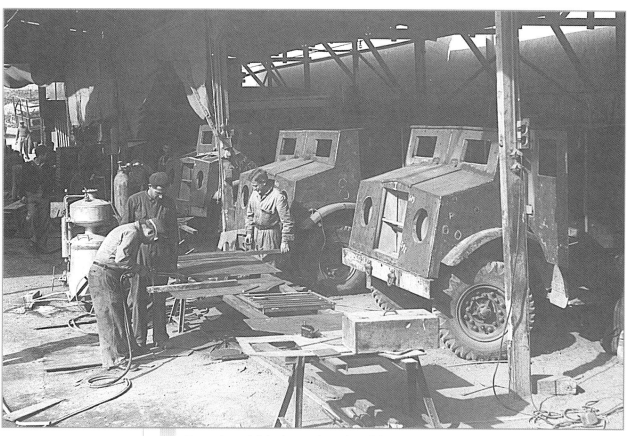

The *Haganah* established a number of workshops to produce armoured vehicles in anticipation of the inevitable war to be fought to preserve the soon-to-be declared State of Israel. This is the *Ha'Argaz* shop in Tel Aviv in March 1948, with workmen building several identical armoured lorries. The base vehicles appear to be CMP pattern 15 cwt lorries with Cab No. 13. *(Kluger Zoltan, Israeli Government Press Office)*

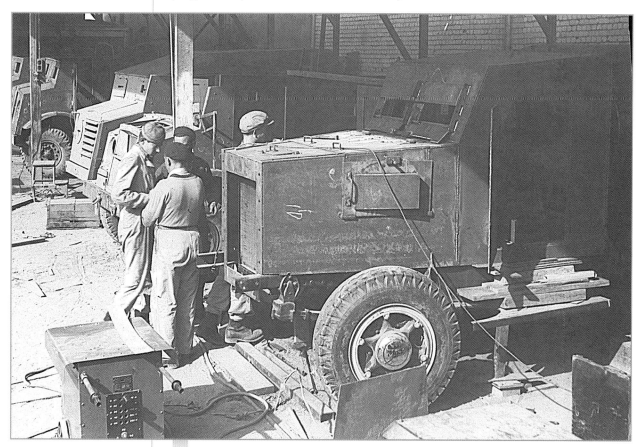

Farther to the right down the line, one of the CMP conversions looks complete and another is nearly so. They are also converting a civilian lorry. *(Kluger Zoltan, Israeli Government Press Office)*

Some of the CMP conversions, probably for carrying cargo, had soft tops. The old Italeri reissue of the Peerless CMP Quad gun tractor is ideal for this type of vehicle. The makeshift nature of the armour is evident around the door window. *(Kluger Zoltan, Israeli Government Press Office)*

This particular vehicle is very different from the others built at the *Ha'Argaz* factory. It is impossible to determine the base vehicle, but it is larger than the previous one, possibly a CMP 3-ton lorry. It may have a sloped roof with a canvas cover over the "butterfly wing" type wire mesh hatches. The colour is noticeably lighter than olive drab, so it could be a sand shade. *(Kluger Zoltan, Israeli Government Press Office)*

Early in the War of Independence, on 14th June 1948, this CMP pattern sandwich truck needs a little help from a bulldozer to climb a hill on the "Burma Road". This road was built to bypass the main Tel Aviv-Jerusalem road, which was constantly subject to attack by Arab forces. A portion of this road still exists today. The wide white band is left over from the pre-war period, when it was required by the British to distinguish between Jewish and Arab vehicles. *(Pinn Hans, Israeli Government Press Office)*

This photograph may be posed: this does not seem to be the most advantageous way to exit the vehicle, except in an emergency. There is a rear door, in addition to the two in front. This is another of the sandwich trucks that entered service before the declaration of the State of Israel. It, too, has the white identification stripe required by the British. The Hebrew lettering is roughly translated to mean "Trouble Free". *(Israeli Government Press Office)*

These CMP sandwich trucks are open-topped personnel carriers with firing ports. Battering rams to break through Arab roadblocks were common features on the early *Haganah* lorries, and they can still be seen on all types of vehicles from Main Battle Tanks to lorries and M113s today. *(Israeli Government Press Office)*

This is a slightly different design, but still based on a Canadian Military Pattern lorry. The radiator is just barely visible behind the massive looking bars. Nicknamed "Monster", this vehicle was used in the northern part of Israel. The armour plate was installed at Kibbutz Kfar Giladi. *(David Levy)*

The battering ram was a rather simple design. When lowered, the skid ran along the road surface. The whole rig was fabricated from simple angle iron. This series of all around photographs provides enough information for the modeller to build one of these unique lorries. Italeri re-released the old Peerless/Max Quad gun tractor, and they also have a cargo lorry version. *(David Levy)*

The ram was raised and lowered using a simple pulley system operated from the cargo bed. *(David Levy)*

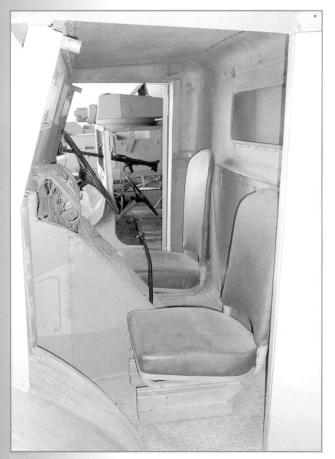

The original softskin cab is intact inside the armour plating. Visible through the open cab is a Jeep configured like one of the vehicles used by Samson's Foxes in 1948. Beyond it is a Marmon-Herrington Mark IV (minus its turret) and a Humber armoured car without a gun. *(David Levy)*

The vision slits are protected by simple sliding doors. Note the thickness of the armour. This CMP vehicle has right-hand drive. *(David Levy)*

This is the hand crank used to lower and raise the ram. *(David Levy)*

The construction of this lorry is quite plain, but the photographer believes that it is an original sandwich truck, recently restored for this display at the Collection Houses. *(David Levy)*

Just like the older lorry shown previously, access to the armoured body was through a simple door in the cargo bed. The round objects are plough discs that have been cut down and used here to provide firing apertures and head protection for the crew. *(David Levy)*

The sandwich plates in this example are hollow. The wood may have rotted and been removed, or, perhaps, the gaps were filled with sand or dirt. *(David Levy)*

This is a photograph of a picture hanging on the shed wall. The image appears less than lifelike due to distortion caused by light on the glass. The vehicle is actually reflected in the glass. The construction of this cab is cruder than that of the display vehicle. *(David Levy)*

Sandwich Trucks

This scene is from before the War of Independence. These two sandwich trucks are probably part of the escort for a supply convoy travelling between kibbutzim. Although armed, these are civilians. The ram vehicle differs from those in the previous photographs. Obviously, the design using the plough discs for firing ports was a standard one. *(Mark Hazzard)*

While many of the sandwich trucks appear to be built around the lighter weight classes, this one, on parade on 1st July 1948, is closer to the $2\frac{1}{2}$ to 3-ton variety. The sandwich armour is clearly illustrated by the thickness of the open door. The side armour plates on the engine compartment are lowered, perhaps due to the heat. Note the cartoon markings. *(Israeli Government Press Office)*

The *Palmach* and *Haganah* were consolidated into the new Israeli Defence Force. Their makeshift vehicles continued in use during the War of Independence. This column is part of the Givati Brigade. Today, the Brigade is an elite unit of the IDF, specialising in, among other things, amphibious landings. In 1948, it included the famous Jeep-borne Samson's Foxes. The lorry behind the Jeep is very similar in style to the one in the previous photograph, although this one has a sloped roof and wire mesh hatches. It is followed by a couple of the CMP conversions. *(Kluger Zoltan, Israeli Government Press Office)*

This obviously posed photograph is dated 12th June 1948. It is a good example of a sandwich truck, the same one as in the previous image, showing how the crew would fight from it. Note the collection of British helmets and the ex-Czech 98K rifles. *(Kluger Zoltan, Israeli Government Press Office)*

This is the right side of the same vehicle. The screens obviously were only useful for deflecting grenades and debris. The crew is armed with 98K rifles and a Bren gun. *(Kluger Zoltan, Israeli Government Press Office)*

According to the original caption, this is a training exercise, unit unknown, in the Judean hills near Jerusalem. The date is 25th November 1948. The vehicle is one of the longer ones, possibly based on an American-built chassis, such as a $2\frac{1}{2}$ ton GMC, or a civilian vehicle. The smoke obscures the rear wheels, so it is impossible to see if it has a single or double axle. *(Israeli Government Press Office)*

The crew of this sandwich truck is unloading supplies near Jerusalem. The original caption is dated October 1948. Although the Judean hills would possibly be a little cooler at that time of year, the shorts and sleeves indicate that it is still quite warm. Note the soldier on the left is armed with a 98K rifle. The uniforms are a combination of military and civilian items. *(Israeli Government Press Office)*

Photographed in 1949, this sandwich truck has seen better days. The added weight of the composite armour put a lot of extra strain on the engines and chassis. Due to the suspension parts lying around, this vehicle was likely under repair before it was abandoned, somewhere in the Negev Desert. *(Kluger Zoltan, Israeli Government Press Office)*

Sandwich Trucks

This vehicle is also abandoned in the Negev. It has been stripped and placed on blocks. Although a desert, the Negev is not all sand. *(Kluger Zoltan, Israeli Government Press Office)*

According to the original caption, this is a destroyed Syrian vehicle. It definitely does not follow the common Israeli practice of armouring the entire vehicle. There also appears to be an open area in the rear. The lorry was hit during the fighting for Kibbutz Degania Alef, near the Sea of Galilee. *(Kluger Zoltan, Israeli Government Press Office)*

All sorts of vehicles were modified for use at the widely scattered kibbutzim and along the roads in between. This one resembles a road maintenance vehicle with its extended cab. Its origins may have been a construction vehicle, perhaps a dump truck. Although it is a rather crude-looking conversion, it is still in use during the battle for Beersheba in the Negev in October 1948. *(Israeli Government Press Office)*

Egypt captured this sandwich truck, but lost it again in the battle for Beersheba in October 1948. The Egyptian roundel has been superimposed over the white identification stripe left over from the British Mandate. The IDF soldier appears to be firing at an aircraft. *(Israeli Government Press Office)*

This front view of the same vehicle identifies it as a conversion from a British- or Canadian-built lorry, probably a 3-ton CMP No. 12 cab. The latter's shape would account for the sloping side panels on the bonnet (hood for those in the United States). *(Hugo Mendelson, Israeli Government Press Office)*

Egypt retains this captured sandwich truck, however. It is on display at the museum at El Alamein. It is also a 3-ton long wheel base CMP No. 12 cab conversion, either a Chevrolet C60L or a Ford F60L. Note that the armour construction is partly welded and partly riveted. *(Mark Hazzard)*

Note that the passenger side windscreen has an additional cutout to allow a weapon to be fired. Although Canadians drive on the right side of the road, many of these trucks were built with right-hand drive for use by the British, who drive on the left side. The headlight covers are hinged and can be raised for driving in non-blackout conditions. (This distinguished-looking gentleman is a good friend of the author's, Mark Hazzard from the United Kingdom. Mark's shirt doubles as an advertisement for the non-commercial Miniature Armoured Fighting Vehicles Association). *(Mark Hazzard)*

As with some other surviving sandwich trucks, the filler material for the sandwich is missing. The crude, yet effective, nature of the construction is evident, however. *(Mark Hazzard)*

The armoured covers on the door windows were opened by sliding the flap down, rather than being hinged. The door latch is also quite basic in design. *(Mark Hazzard)*

The single rear door is very similar in its construction. These sandwich trucks were simple, yet effective, designs. *(Mark Hazzard)*

The seat behind the wheel well almost looks like a lounge chair. Even after all these years, some of the fabric covering remains intact. Note that the firing ports have covers that flip up on a hinge pin. The opening in the roof was normally covered by hinged screens, leaving the interior open to the elements. *(Mark Hazzard)*

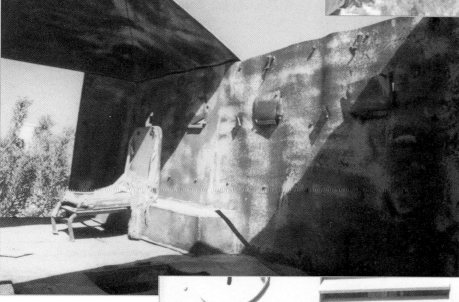

This particular vehicle has four-wheel drive. This was not true for all sandwich trucks, as can be seen with the soft-top vehicle shown previously. *(Mark Hazzard)*

Construction was based on commercial manufacturing techniques. The armoured body is mounted to the chassis using U-bolts. Even though the basic lorry is very definitely a military design, commercial tyres were commonly used. This was true for all types of IDF vehicles, from Jeeps to half-tracks, for decades. *(Mark Hazzard)*

This view shows not only the U-bolt construction, but also the fact that the metal sheathing was fabricated from multiple plates welded together. The vehicle visible beyond the sandwich truck is a derelict M2 half-track. *(Mark Hazzard)*

This detached sandwich truck body is on display at the IDF Collection Houses in Tel Aviv-Jaffa. It appears to be the victim of a mine explosion. Obviously, it is impossible to tell what type of lorry was used for the conversion. *(Mark Hazzard)*

This version was fitted with double doors at the rear. Most of the others had only one. The force of the mine explosion blew off the front portion of the roof as well. The thickness of the armour is evident in the firing ports. Also visible are the braces for a bench seat over the wheel well, and hinges for a side mudguard. *(Mark Hazzard)*

The vehicle obviously suffered a catastrophic explosion to the cab area. Braces for a bench seat are visible on this side as well. Note that firing port doors slide on this version. There is absolutely no overhead protection from an air burst. The screens would only deflect a grenade, which would then, hopefully, explode away from the vehicle.

This armoured truck probably served as a troop carrier escorting supply convoys. The layout resembles that of the US half-track series, including a rear door. It is impossible to determine the base vehicle, but it could possibly be a US Chevrolet $2\frac{1}{2}$ ton or similar. These troops are preparing to move forward during Operation Horev on 12th December 1948. *(Israeli Government Press Office)*

This later, more compact, sandwich truck is built on a modified Dodge $\frac{3}{4}$ ton Weapons Carrier chassis. In this right front three-quarter view, the 'butterfly'-type roof hatch, also a feature of the earlier sandwich trucks, is visible.

Left front three-quarter view of the same vehicle. Although somewhat reminiscent of the crude armoured cars from the 1920s, it is quite well constructed. There are armoured louvres for the front and sides of the engine compartment, and armoured flaps for the driver and co-driver.

This is the left side showing the firing slits all around. Each has a sliding door on the inside of the truck. The mudguards are hinged to allow access to the tyre. The left side flap also includes a small hinged door for the fuel filler cap.

This is a view forward from the open rear door. Visible are the sliding flaps for the right side firing slits, and a bench for the crew.

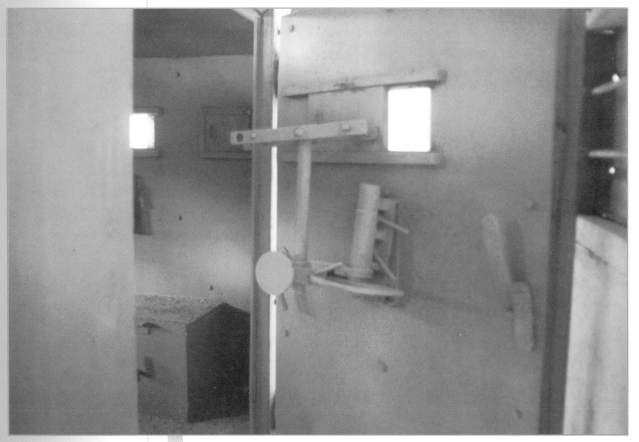

The composite "sandwich" construction is very evident in this view. There is wood between two sheets of steel on the body and the door. The odd-looking mechanism on the door may be a mount for a light machine gun; it is a feature common to other similar hulls on display elsewhere. (Mark Hazzard)

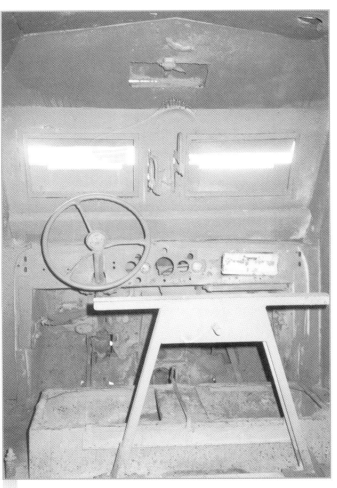

The interior of the vehicle is not quite as well maintained as the exterior. The seats, controls and instrument panel are standard Dodge features. The metal stand behind the seats is a firing step for shooting through the small hatch in the front slope of the roof.

Again, the "sandwich" nature of the armour is evident is this view of the driver's door. Note that the armoured window cover slides to open and close. However, this one is mounted the opposite way from that on the passenger door. *(Mark Hazzard)*

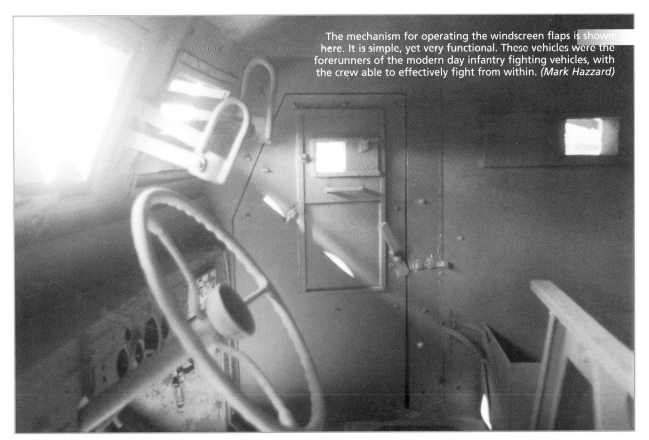

The mechanism for operating the windscreen flaps is shown here. It is simple, yet very functional. These vehicles were the forerunners of the modern day infantry fighting vehicles, with the crew able to effectively fight from within. *(Mark Hazzard)*

The Dodge conversion was a common one. There are several of them displayed along the motorway from Tel Aviv to Jerusalem, like the one on the right in this photograph. The centre shell has since been relocated. It is the armoured cab from an otherwise unarmoured supply lorry. The CMP vehicle on the left is shown again at the end of this section. *(Sa'Ar Ya'Acov, Israeli Government Press Office)*

This is a rear view of the same Dodge-based vehicle. These vehicles were originally left where they were knocked out, to serve as memorials to the people who had died defending the supply convoys to Jerusalem. When a new modern motorway was built a short distance from the old road, the remains were relocated to the new one. The wood portion of the door armour has long since rotted away, or been accidentally lost in transit from the old location. *(Mark Hazzard)*

This is the interior of same vehicle. *(Mark Hazzard)*

This is the left side of the same vehicle, but in a different location. The roof hatches were built high enough to allow a man to stand and fire both to the front and the rear, without exposing himself. Note the flap for the fuel filler cap. The protruding object in front of the roof hatch is just a pine cone. *(Mark Hazzard)*

The same hull was moved, again. As of May 2005, it sits in the median of the dual carriageway near Jerusalem, with other vehicles. A section of the old "Burma Road" is not too far from this location. *(Josh Weingarten)*

This right-side view will be very useful for the model builder. An interesting feature is that the torch-cut ports are not symmetrical, or even cut straight. *(Josh Weingarten)*

This rear view of the third vehicle shows the rear door hinges, and another non-rectangular firing port. Another difference between this design and the earlier sandwich trucks is the use of solid roof hatches. *(Mark Hazzard)*

The rear door is closed on this example. *(Mark Hazzard)*

This vehicle is very similar in layout and design to the Dodge conversion. The louvres and door are different, however. It is located not far from the other vehicles in this series of photographs. *(Mark Hazzard)*

This appears to be a right-hand drive lorry, so it is British in origin. The roof is a little higher than the Dodge. Note that the bonnet has a slight angle downward to the sides. The front roof hatch is present, showing the brace for attaching a rope or chain to close it from the inside. *(Mark Hazzard)*

The vehicle had a single rear axle, which limits the choices for its origin, but it is still impossible to identify it for certain. Any two or three tonner with a long engine compartment with side ventilation may qualify. It could also be based on a commercial lorry. *(Mark Hazzard)*

This armoured car is also based on the Dodge $\frac{3}{4}$ ton ton Weapons Carrier. It is similar in style and layout to the converted M3 scout cars also extensively used during this period. However, the body is narrower, requiring the addition of mudguards over the rear wheels.

Right side of same vehicle. Note that the door is offset to the rear to allow clearance for the turret. Only the driver's visor opens all the way. The right side has a view slit for the turret gunner/co-driver. The bracket is for a fire-extinguisher.

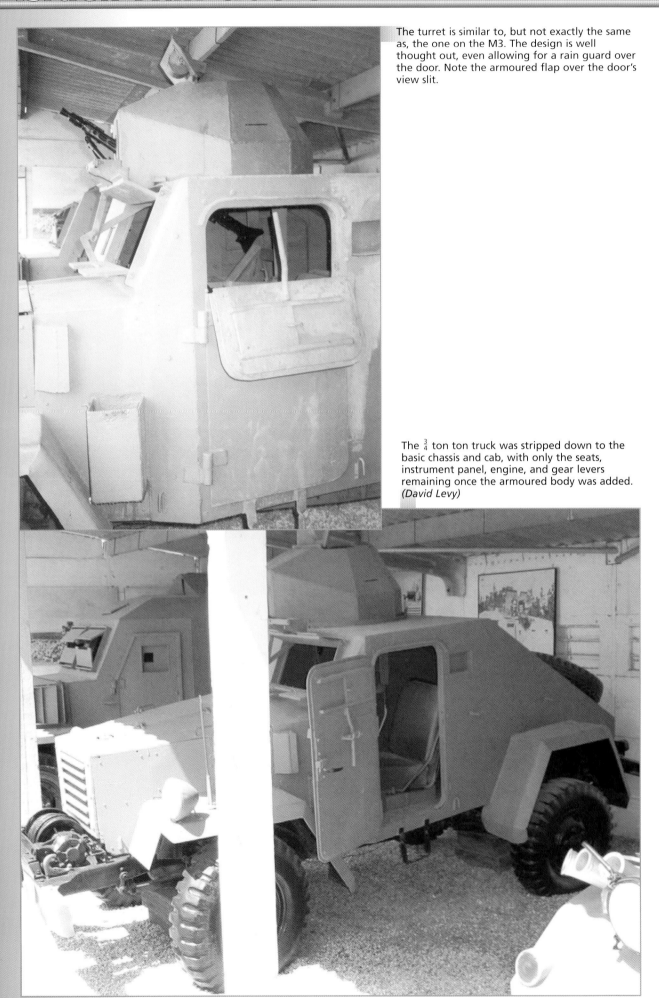

The turret is similar to, but not exactly the same as, the one on the M3. The design is well thought out, even allowing for a rain guard over the door. Note the armoured flap over the door's view slit.

The $\frac{3}{4}$ ton ton truck was stripped down to the basic chassis and cab, with only the seats, instrument panel, engine, and gear levers remaining once the armoured body was added. *(David Levy)*

The driver's side interior is very bare. The door is closed and latched; yet there is still a gap around it. *(David Levy)*

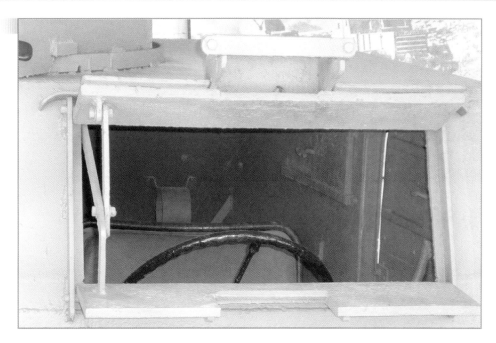

The turret accommodations are quite simple. Since it was not powered, the gunner would have to walk himself around to traverse it. The chain is probably just to secure the exhibit. *(David Levy)*

The bottom half of the hatch closed first, then the top part. The view port overlapped the bottom. *(David Levy)*

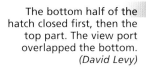

This view shows the covers closed. The bipod on the MG 34 is non-standard, probably because the gun was convenient for the display. There are a several sheds in this collection that are devoted to small arms and personal equipment. There is even a building to display Arab items, including PLO equipment. *(Mark Hazzard)*

Left side at the rear. The slope is quite severe, leaving little room for any movement inside toward the rear. However, there is a view port, firing slit in the bulkhead.

Right side rear view. The offset door is really obvious here. Across the way is one of several buildings filled with exhibits covering everything from IDF uniforms and field gear to PLO weapons. Some vehicles are under cover in open air sheds, while others are in the open. However, they are all in very good condition. *(David Levy)*

The next two photographs are useful for anyone wanting to build the turret. Even though these vehicles were homegrown, the welding is high quality. *(Mark Hazzard)*

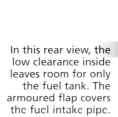

This view shows the placement of the turret relative to the sides. It is a very compact vehicle, unlike the roomier vehicles shown previously. *(Mark Hazzard)*

In this rear view, the low clearance inside leaves room for only the fuel tank. The armoured flap covers the fuel intake pipe.

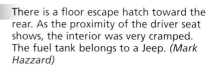

There is a floor escape hatch toward the rear. As the proximity of the driver seat shows, the interior was very cramped. The fuel tank belongs to a Jeep. *(Mark Hazzard)*

One of these armoured cars leads a converted M3 Scout Car ahead of other vehicles in a convoy in the Judean Mountains on 1st October 1948. The lead vehicle has a few minor detail differences from the one in the previous photograph series, but it is clearly of the same class and design. Note that there were several different turret designs in use. *(Israeli Government Press Office)*

This is the same armoured car, with a machine gun in the co-driver firing port. As can be seen from this series of photographs, this particular convoy had a range of different types of vehicle, which would be typical for the IDF at the time. At some point, vehicles changed their respective places in line. *(Israeli Government Press Office)*

This vehicle is similar to the one in the previous photographs. There are subtle differences, however. This armoured lorry is part of the 79th Armoured Battalion, stationed in the northern part of the country. The battalion included two companies of these vehicles, plus two more equipped with half-tracks. *(Ralph Lowenstein)*

This conversion, Identification Number 10624, is on a vehicle with right-hand drive. At a glance, it looks much like the Canadian-built Otter Mark 1, but it is larger. The general shape of the armour resembles the Morris Commercial 8 cwt chassis, but the bumper looks like that on the CMP Cab No.12 8 cwt lorry. The generally relaxed attitude suggests that danger is not imminent, but one soldier is taking aim through a scope on his Enfield rifle. His companion is discussing the situation on a US Second World War-era walkie-talkie. He is carrying a Thompson sub-machine gun. *(Israeli Government Press Office)*

This, however, is indeed an Otter Mark 1. It was re-fitted with a standard IDF turret. Its crew is preparing to take part in Operation Horev. *(Israeli Government Press Office)*

The same vehicle is seen here as part of a group of vehicles in Chalutza, in the Negev, December 1948. *(Israeli Government Press Office)*

This upgraded Otter is entering Ein Kerem near Jerusalem in October 1948. Given the very relaxed posture of the vehicle commander, hostilities in the area are over. These Canadian-built vehicles had right-hand drive, so the co-driver's machine gun is on the left. *(Israeli Government Press Office)*

A wrecker based on a CMP Chevrolet is seen here towing No. 10624, which seems to have developed a problem. Note the various angles and shape of the rear armour, relative to the other conversions. The scene is also in the Judean hills near Jerusalem on 1st October 1948. *(Israeli Government Press Office)*

This is the same vehicle from the other side, and the problem is clearly with the left-rear wheel. The design of the rear portion is very similar to that used on the Dodge $\frac{3}{4}$ ton Weapons Carrier, but the front is very different. *(Israeli Government Press Office)*

Farther back in the column is yet another style, again similar but not identical. This one is higher, with the roof sloping up and back from the windscreen. The bonnet is higher, with large side louvres. It also appears to be British or Commonwealth in origin, but the exact type is unknown. *(Israeli Government Press Office)*

A similar vehicle is seen at Kfar Qasim, following the transfer of authority from Trans-Jordan to Israel in May 1949. This armoured car's bumper is different from that in the previous photograph, confirming that the type was built in some quantity like the other types. *(Israeli Government Press Office)*

This is the rear of the same vehicle. Compare this with the rear view of the towed armoured car in the previous photographs. *(Israeli Government Press Office)*

The armoured lorry on the left is probably based on the same right-hand drive vehicle as the one in the previous series. The sandwich truck on the right is an open-topped personnel carrier very similar – but not identical to – the one in the parade shown earlier. Not being able to see the front of the vehicle, the main visible difference appears to be the cutout at the rear corner. It may also be a little shorter. *(Israeli Government Press Office)*

This column in the Judean hills near Jerusalem has apparently come under fire. Besides several converted armoured cars, there is a South African-built Marmon-Herrington Armoured Reconnaissance Car Mark IV. In the original print, the converted lorry in the foreground has some sort of artwork done in what appears to be white chalk. There are obviously several similar yet distinctly different designs for these conversions. After all, while they followed several common designs, each was built individually by hand, in different workshops. The date is 1st October 1948. *(Israeli Government Press Office)*

This is a close-up of a vehicle similar in design to that in the previous photograph. The hull angles are the same, distinctly more vertical than on the other designs. The rear slope is covered by a sheet of canvas or other heavy cloth. The photograph is posed. Note that the standing figure is carrying a Sten gun with no magazine, but he has a belt of machine gun ammunition around his neck and a cartridge belt that looks American in origin. The uniform is also a mix of British and American items. *(Ralph Lowenstein)*

A column of camouflaged vehicles from the 8th Brigade moves forward. The first armoured car is a converted lorry, followed by two converted White M3 Scout Cars. *(Kluger Zoltan, Israeli Government Press Office)*

This armoured car is advancing toward Beersheba in 1948. It is another indication that multiple styles existed for these conversions. Whether this is one of a kind is unknown. The rear is tilted slightly forward from vertical and is fitted with a large access door, unlike the others shown. It has two antennae, so the altered design may be intentional for a command vehicle. Note the desolate nature of the Negev, as well as the stone markers along the roadside. *(Eldan David, Israeli Government Press Office)*

At first glance, this appears to be based on the Otter. However, it is too high. The entire vehicle is large, with a different side door arrangement than those shown previously. Note the armoured hatch in the door. It looks like there may be glass in the driver's window, which, with the relaxed appearance of the troops, means this is not a combat situation. With the bipods fitted to the MG 34 machine guns, it is unlikely that the there is a ball mount in either position. *(Israeli Government Press Office)*

The commander/gunner of a converted M3 Scout Car gives orders to troops near Abu Agela during Operation Horev (also known as "Chorev") on 15th December 1948. Readers of the author's *The Israeli Sherman* book will recall that the first IDF Sherman casualty, "Tamar", met its demise at El Arish during this campaign, the purpose of which was to drive the Egyptians from the Sinai. *(Israeli Government Press Office)*

This is an excellent rare overhead view of one of the converted M3 Scout Cars. It is 10th October 1948 in Jaffa, near Tel Aviv, and the military police are preparing to enforce a curfew. Today, the city is often referred to as Tel Aviv-Jaffa. Jaffa is the older section, with a large open-air market, very narrow streets, a restored area with artists and quaint shops and the IDF Collection Houses. (It is quite a contrast standing next to a market stall with recently plucked dead chickens hanging on a line, with a view of the seaside high-rise hotels just a short distance away). *(Israeli Government Press Office)*

This converted M3 sits outside a stable or barn, awaiting its next action. It has a tactical marking on the turret, not often seen on these vehicles. *(Ralph Lowenstein)*

Following the fighting around and through Kibbutz Beit Eshel, these vehicles have been covered with a camouflage net. The vehicle on the left is a Morris Light Reconnaissance Car Mark II – possibly left behind when the British evacuated the previous spring. The crew of the converted M3 Scout Car has removed the MG 34s, possibly to use them in a defence perimeter. *(Israeli Government Press Office)*

A column of converted M3s drives down a road in the Egyptian desert during Operation Horev. The degree of standardisation, even at this early stage, is very evident. The vehicle in the foreground appears to be a half-track rather than a standard M3 Scout Car. Period photographs support the theory that all of the early IDF half-tracks were of the IHC variety, but they did not come standard with a skate rail for machine guns. At the same time, the rail-equipped M2s and M4s did not have the framework around the top, with the rail serving its purpose. Consequently, this could be an IHC vehicle with an improvised rail. The extra antennae indicate a command vehicle. *(Israeli Government Press Office)*

Israeli troops hold an Egyptian prisoner-of-war at Auga El Chafir, 10th December 1948. Visible are two M3 Scout Cars, one of the previously mentioned armoured cars built on a right-hand drive lorry and, in the background, a Marmon-Herrington Mark IV. Note the brown Soviet-style tanker helmets, manufactured in Czechoslovakia. *(Israeli Government Press Office)*

This is the same unit, seen from the other side of the column. In the rear is another of the larger armoured car conversions. This town served as IDF headquarters during Operation Horev. *(Israeli Government Press Office)*

The original caption, dated 10th December 1948, states that these troops have spotted Egyptian Spitfires. The subject of their attention appears, however, to be closer to ground level. They also do not seem to be alarmed at the prospect of being strafed, at least in the near future. The commander of the converted Scout Car is speaking to someone rather casually as well. *(Israeli Government Press Office)*

It is 15th December 1948 in the Negev, and this converted M3 Scout Car is obviously having some engine problems. Buses in Israel have always served double duty as troop transports, so it is no surprise to see them in that role here. *(Israeli Government Press Office)*

Just before the fighting in the Egyptian desert begins, the crew of this converted M3 Scout Car prepares a meal. The armoured car is covered in a camouflage net. Note that a member of the crew is a female. *(Israeli Government Press Office)*

This may be the same female crewman as seen in the previous photograph. The image illustrates very clearly the method of construction for the co-driver's machine gun. Note the quality of the welding work. It is also quite obvious that the desert can be cold. *(Israeli Government Press Office)*

משוריין תש"ח

משוריין "סנדביץ" ממלחמת
העצמאות שימש ללווי
שיירות ופריצת הדרך
לירושלים.

There are no surviving converted M3s at the Collection Houses, nor in any other known location for that matter. This shell is on display at the Monument to the Fallen of the "Har El" Brigade at Har Adar. This is otherwise known as "Radar Hill", in the hills near Jerusalem. (It is very easy to find: coming from Jerusalem, turn right at the Elvis Inn. This roadside restaurant has the largest collection of Elvis Presley memorabilia outside of Memphis – according to the owners, that is. They may very well be right. Just look for the large statue of "The King").

There are many M3 Scout Cars in private hands around the world. Perhaps someone associated with the Latrun museum will find one someday to put under this shell. *(Mark Hazzard)*

The area forward of the windscreen has been added for display purposes. Also on display here are a M51 Sherman (detailed in the book *The Israeli Sherman*), an ex-Jordanian M47 Patton, an early Centurion, a Jeep and a half-track. The Centurion was acquired from The Netherlands, but never used by the Israelis).

Compare this view with the column of M3s shown previously. The early Centurion Mark 5, nicknamed "Hush Puppy" by the Israelis, is fitted with a 20-pounder with Type A barrel. The monument is surrounded by a very well-to-do housing development, and there is an extensive array of radio or telecommunication towers and antennae nearby.

The turret on the converted scout car was installed far enough back, and the body was wide enough, that the side doors did not have to be staggered. To the left is a stone bunker, one of several which, along with a number of slit trenches, formed this position from the War of Independence.

The turret was slightly offset to the right, as is evident in this and the following photograph. The prominence of the hilltop position is obvious, with the houses in the distance. The view is the same all around.

The tower in the background allows for an even more impressive view of the hills near Jerusalem. A slit trench is visible next to the Centurion. Visitors can walk through the bunkers as well. Note the pitting on the armour plate.

Compare this photograph with the overhead view of the vehicle in service in October 1948. It appears as though this turret is sitting just a little too far to the rear. *(Mark Hazzard)*

A close examination of the photograph will show that even these conversions were built with sandwich type armour. The lower portion, of course, is the original armour plate of the basic M3. Above that, beginning at the point where it slopes inward, is the wood from the sandwich armour. The inside metal sheet is partially missing from this view. However, the wood itself is very obvious. The rack in front of the wheel well is a rifle rack, possibly remaining from the original Scout Car. *(Mark Hazzard)*

The sandwich armour is much more obvious in this photograph. Note the brackets for bench seats at the rear and along the sides. The familiar sliding doors for the firing ports are here as well. An escape hatch has been added to the floor. *(Mark Hazzard)*

Perhaps this vehicle is the one in the accompanying photographs? It is difficult to confirm. Compare the periscope, hatch and driver's visor to the opening on the hulk at Har Adar. Female soldiers were a common sight during the War of Independence. *(Israeli Government Press Office)*

This view of the same armoured car confirms that it is a converted Scout Car. It is part of a column preparing for Operation Horev and obviously it is cold in the desert in the winter. Note the marking for Southern Command: three forward pointing arrows. Compare the periscope, hatch and driver's visor to the opening on the hulk at Har Adar. *(Israeli Government Press Office)*

19th April 1949 is Liberation Day in Haifa. This column of armoured vehicles includes a couple of converted M3 Scout Cars and a South African-built Marmon-Herrington Mark IV armoured car. Note the glass windscreen in place on the first vehicle. *(Teddy Brauner, Israeli Government Press Office)*

This is yet another body style on a converted M3 Scout Car. The rear lacks the severe slope, and the cab is higher as well. It has the usual ball-mounted machine gun, and this one has an armoured flap above it. Another MG 34 is now mounted on the turret top. The occasion is the Liberation Day parade in Haifa on 19th April 1949, which explains the whitewall tyres. *(Israeli Government Press Office)*

This is a distinctly different vehicle, with a similar body style that indicates it may be an additional standard type. However, it does not appear to have the small hatch just above the front machine gun, as seen in the previous photograph. *(Israeli Government Press Office)*

This is the Army Day parade in Tel Aviv, 17th July 1949. The modified M3 is missing the front roller, which was common but not universal with these conversions. The next two vehicles are Otter Mark 1s that have been upgraded with larger turrets. The lower sides of these turrets are not vertical. *(Eldan David, Israeli Government Press Office)*

The original Hebrew caption gives a date of 1948. Given the casual appearance of the troops and the warm weather clothing, the actual date must be either during the summer of 1948, between battles, or while on a patrol in the spring or summer of 1949. The first vehicle is interesting in that, although it is very obviously a converted Scout Car, it has non-standard sheet metal mudguards. Note the markings, which appear to be in chalk. Comparing the various vehicles in this series of photographs, there are some minor differences in what is essentially a standard. This is noticeable around the doors and on the armoured flaps over the windscreen. *(IDF Archives, Ministry of Defence)*

Although, at first glance, this looks like a civilian girl, it is actually a posed shot of a *Chen* (Female Army) member. Note the cartridge belt and walkie-talkie. She is sitting on top of one of the standard machine gun turrets installed on the many types of upgraded or converted armoured cars. There were slight differences between several similar styles. Note the welds and the detail of the ball mount for the covered MG 34. Some Israeli sources refer to these guns as "Spandau". *(Israeli Government Press Office)*

There are at least five of the converted M3 Scout Cars in this photograph taken in front of the Lydda airport, between Tel Aviv and Jerusalem. This airport is also known, interchangeably, as Lod Airport. Its modern incarnation is Ben Gurion International. Other armour involved in the action to capture this transportation link to the outside included the H39 tanks of the 82nd Tank Battalion's "Russian Company", so called because its members were immigrants from the Soviet Union. The "English Company" of the 82nd operated Cromwell and Sherman tanks. *(Israeli Government Press Office via the wall at the Collection Houses, via Mark Hazzard)*

The force that captured Lod Airport was a mixed bag, typical of the IDF at the time. Two of the Hotchkiss H39 light tanks flank one of the converted lorries. Although it is a distant shot, this appears to be the same style as the vehicle preserved at The IDF Collection Houses in Tel Aviv-Jaffa. One of the H39s is on display at Latrun. A very small swastika stamped on the hull front confirms that it at one time served with the German forces in the Second World War. *(Israeli Government Press Office)*

Although some of the vehicles are covered and are far from the camera, it is possible to identify several different types. In the foreground, from left to right, are two converted M3 Scout Cars, a captured Humber armoured car with Egyptian markings, one of the turreted IHC M5 half-tracks with the 20 mm gun and another converted M3 Scout Car. In the background, from the left, are a converted M3 Scout Car, and then another Humber armoured car, an unmodified Otter Mark I and finally another M3 Scout Car. The scene is in the desert near El Manshafra on 15th December 1948, during Operation Horev. (Israeli Government Press Office)

This group of armoured vehicles is advancing into Egyptian territory during Operation Horev. The photograph, although not of the best quality, shows several interesting things. The converted Scout Car in the foreground has odd front mudguards, either damaged or fabricated from flat plates. The third vehicle is an unconverted M3 Scout Car. The turret above it is actually on a fourth vehicle. *(Israeli Government Press Office)*

The Egyptian Army garrison at Abu Agela in the Sinai, December 1948, surrendered and more or less effectively brought an end to the War of Independence. There are two distinctly different looking converted lorries shown here. They could both be $\frac{3}{4}$ ton Dodge Weapons Carriers, but the body styles are different. *(Israeli Government Press Office)*

This is the same unit as in the previous photograph. In fact, this is likely the same armoured car as shown to the right. It clearly shows that the interior is painted white. The exterior is probably a shade of olive drab. The infantryman is distinctly British looking, but he carries the very common 98K rifle obtained from Czechoslovakia. *(Israeli Government Press Office)*

The quality and clarity of this photograph is particularly poor. However, it was chosen for publication because it shows what appears to be yet another small converted armoured car. It is driving away from the photographer, with its turret traversed to the rear. What makes it unusual is that it appears to have a larger open door or hatch in the rear slope. The action takes place during the battle for Abu Agela in December 1948. *(Israeli Government Press Office)*

The modern dual carriageway from Tel Aviv to Jerusalem is not too far away from the old road, along which many battles were fought. When the new road was built, the Israelis re-located some of the destroyed vehicles. All that remains are the armour shells and perhaps an occasional chassis. These last two photographs show the variety of body styles in use. This particular type is not one of the more common ones; it appears to be an armoured cab for a supply truck. *(Ohayon Avi, Israeli Government Press Office)*

All of these monument vehicles are painted in bright red primer, lining both sides of the motorway on the approach to Jerusalem. This CMP vehicle looks like it was a wrecker, similar to the one shown previously, although this one has an armoured cab. *(Sa'Ar Ya'Acov, Israeli Government Press Office)*

A closer view further reinforces the potential that this is a wrecker. This appears to be the base for the lift crane. The storage bins would hold various tools and chain. *(Josh Weingarten)*

The crudeness of the construction on this supply lorry is a testament to the bravery of the people that used these vehicles. The base vehicle is an old light-duty civilian lorry. It is presently located in the median of the Tel Aviv/Jerusalem dual carriageway. *(Josh Weingarten)*

Aside from the memorials along the roads, the Israelis made a concerted effort to preserve the history of the early makeshift armour force. A 1948-era sandwich truck is driven around Hebrew University stadium during the 1978 Independence Day celebration. It is very similar to the vehicle on display in Tel Aviv, including the paint and marking scheme. It also appears to be built on an American chassis, although it may be a reproduction: without seeing it up close, it is impossible to say for sure. If it is, it is a very good one. *(Milner Moshe, Israeli Government Press Office)*

This vehicle, on display at Latrun, is definitely a mock-up. From a distance, it looks real; however, up-close, the recent construction is very evident. Even so, it is an excellent rendition of a sandwich truck.

This vehicle is also a reproduction, of the same high quality as the one at Latrun. This one is at the Givati Brigade museum in the south. (Josh Weingarten)

Chapter Three Armoured Cars

This may very well be the first of several Daimler Armoured Car Mark Is acquired during the war. This one still carries British markings, so it is likely one that was appropriated from them as they were leaving Palestine. It is taking part in some sort of parade, probably during the summer of 1948. *(Ralph Lowenstein)*

Small numbers of standard armoured cars were acquired, through direct purchase and capture. Taking part in the Liberation Day parade in Haifa in April 1949 are a Daimler Armoured Car and a South African-produced Marmon-Herrington Armoured Reconnaissance Car Mark IVF. There are several available or published photographs of Daimlers with distinct differences, enough to indicate that several were probably acquired. The first, at least, was "liberated" from the British Police Mobile Force. The unit marking is that of the renowned 7th Armoured Brigade. *(Israeli Government Press Office)*

The original caption states that this scene is during manoeuvres in the Judean hills in November 1948. The Daimler on the right is missing it mudguards, so it is likely that it saw some combat. On the left is one of the conversions on a CMP or other British type lorry. *(Israeli Government Press Office)*

This is a closer view of the Daimler. The missing mudguards drastically change the vehicle's profile. The rear marking is not a standard IDF marking, and looks British in nature. It is probably still in its original paint as well. *(Israeli Government Press Office)*

A Marmon-Herrington Mark IVF leads a column of armoured vehicles toward Beersheba during the war. The British-led Trans-Jordanian Arab Legion, as well as the British themselves, used these in fairly large numbers. Some of the British vehicles in Palestine were even modified to ride on rails in pairs. This vehicle may have been acquired clandestinely or captured. Note the differences between this vehicle and the one in the previous photograph. The most notable, besides the grab handle on the front, is the short-barrelled 37 mm cannon in place of the normal 2-pounder. This may have come from a disabled Syrian Hotchkiss tank. *(Eldan David, Israeli Government Press Office)*

This is a closer view of the Marmon-Herrington Mark IVF shown previously as part of a convoy in the Judean hills. Several of these were captured, or otherwise obtained by the IDF, and used on several fronts. Note the Dodge ambulance in front of the Mark IVF, as well as the buses in the background. Although the turret is traversed, the casual attitude of the soldiers standing around, and the raised engine deck hatch, indicates that there is no immediate danger. *(Israeli Government Press Office)*

This Mark IVF is participating in a parade to celebrate the opening of what was called the "Burma Road". This was a new road constructed around Arab-controlled territory to allow the flow of supplies to Jerusalem. A number of these armoured cars were acquired by the IDF during the war, and put into immediate service. Moshe Dayan, commanding the 89th Mechanised Battalion, used one such captured vehicle as a command car. *(Israeli Government Press Office)*

The Israeli Armoured Corps Memorial and Museum at Latrun is definitely one of the finest collections of armoured vehicles in the world. This is a rare example of a Marmon-Herrington Mark IVF armoured car. Note the differences in the mantlets on all of the vehicles featured here. This particular vehicle is not a veteran of IDF service; the museum acquired it, as a representative example, from Cyprus. (David Levy)

This is the right rear three-quarter view of the same vehicle. (David Levy)

Note that the box is offset to the left of a view slit in the rear of the turret. This row of displays overlooks the museum parking lot, along with farm fields in the distance. The old ex-British police station sits strategically on a hill that dominates the approaches from Tel Aviv to the west. (David Levy)

This portion of the museum grounds is dedicated to the IDF's earlier years. Behind is a Universal Carrier, circa 1948, and behind that is one of the two Cromwells, also circa 1948, and an M1 Sherman, circa 1956.

This is the turret roof on the Mark IVF. There is no cupola, episcopes or periscopes, so the only view for the turret crew is through small slits in the front and sides. *(David Levy)*

This side view is a good indication of the relatively small size of the Mark IVF. For some reason, the hull side hatch is open, yet the opening is plated over. (David Levy)

This is the first in a series of three photographs showing a Mark IVF entering the village of Kfar Qasim in May 1949, and then standing by as Trans-Jordanian troops evacuate the area. This captured armoured car has been fitted with the usual MG 34 to supplement the co-axial .30 calibre Browning. Note the female talking on the radio, and the MP Jeep. *(Israeli Government Press Office)*

The transition was an orderly one under the terms of the Israel/Trans-Jordan Armistice Agreement. The crew seems to have left the armoured car un-attended. *(Israeli Government Press Office)*

The crowd has dispersed, and the crew has returned to their vehicle. The Mark IVF does not have the normal Arab Legion paint scheme, so perhaps it has been repainted and marked by the IDF. Note the United Nations Jeep standing by, along with some IDF infantrymen. *(Israeli Government Press Office)*

Not all of the Mark IVFs survived unscathed. This vehicle has had its turret blown off. It also looks as though it has been repainted olive drab and given an IDF serial number; Arab Legion vehicles carried British style markings. This is somewhere in Jerusalem after the battle for the city, parts of which stayed in Jordanian hands until 1967. *(Pinn Hans, Israeli Government Press Office)*

By Army Day in July 1949, these Mark IVFs, on the left in the photograph, are repainted and marked with the three arrows of Southern Command. This is a parade in Tel Aviv. Also shown is a captured Humber armoured car with very prominent Israeli markings, and at least two of the converted M3 Scout Cars. In the original print, there are two half-tracks behind the Scout Cars. This may show that some units were very heterogeneous, or simply that this is a sample display of vehicles. *(David Eldan, Israeli Government Press Office)*

The IDF acquired thirty Staghound armoured cars during the 1950s. They were in use until sometime after the 1967 Six Day War. In the late 1970s, some or all of them were sold to Nicaragua. These were used in that country's civil war, including one with a pedestal mounted machine in place of the turret. (Photographs show that this country's army is equipped with a lot of Israeli-made items, including helmets and the Israeli-made copy of the FN-FAL rifle. There has even been a rumour that they acquired some M50 Shermans, but the author has not been able to confirm this. If anyone has photographic evidence, please contact the author via the publisher. There is photographic evidence of standard M4 or M4A3 types with the 105 mm howitzer, which were likely acquired directly from the United States, but which were refurbished by Israeli technicians). This group is assigned to another brigade other than the often-photographed 7th. *(Israeli Government Press Office)*

This Staghound on display at Latrun has seen better days. Although there is no evidence of armour penetrations, this vehicle may have been the victim of foul play. (David Levy)

The engine deck doors are missing, as are the two large prominent exhausts on the rear plate. Only the fixed parts of the deck door hinges remain. The right front mudguard appears to be non-standard also. *(David Levy)*

The turret hatches are also missing. It is quite possible that this vehicle suffered an internal explosion. In the absence of a more suitable example, following the sale to Nicaragua, this derelict was pulled from the scrap heap, simply as representative of the type. *(David Levy)*

Although the Staghound and Marmon-Herrington mounted similar weapons, the Staghound was more heavily armoured. It was originally designed according to British specifications, for use in the North African desert. Note the Universal Carrier in the rear, equipped with the flame-thrower. *(David Levy)*

This side view again shows the dilapidated condition of the vehicle. The sandwich truck in the background is not an original. It has been fabricated to illustrate the type, which is a tribute to the museum staff and the effort to preserve history. *(David Levy)*

These Staghounds are participating in the 1954 Independence Day parade in Ramleh. In the original print, there are six vehicles visible in the frame. *(Brauner Teddy, Israeli Government Press Office)*

Taken at Latrun in 1992, this photograph shows a line-up of armoured cars. From the left, there is a Marmon-Herrington Mark IVF, an AML-90, Staghound, Ferret (these may or may not have seen limited service), Universal Carrier, and possibly a Loyd Carrier. Universal Carriers captured from the Egyptians or "acquired" from the departing British saw extensive use during the War of Independence. The Mark IVF has a non-standard turret, and may be the one seen with a dummy gun in a parade in 1978 – still a runner thirty years later.

This photograph was taken at the Collection Houses in 1992. From the left, there is a Humber Scout Car, a Universal Carrier and another Ferret armoured car. The latter were probably captured from the Jordanians. The Humber Scout Car was similar to the Daimler Dingo, but larger.

The IDF captured several Humber armoured cars from Egypt during the 1948 war. They were pressed into service, even while bearing the Egyptian markings. This surviving example is at the Collection Houses in Jaffa. The cannon is missing. Next to it is a turret-less Marmon-Herrington Mark IV. Could this perhaps be the one shown knocked-out in Jerusalem? *(David Levy)*

Perhaps this is the Jerusalem vehicle. It has been fitted with a dummy turret for display purposes. It was a runner, at least through the 1970s, when it was used in parades. Until the acquisition of the Cypriot vehicle, this was the only turreted example of the type available.

Chapter Four Half-tracks, General Use

The popular image of the IDF during its early years is one of a ragtag group with little in the way of standardisation or discipline; however, that impression is not entirely accurate. Except for the Hebrew writing and the IDF serial number, this could be any group of British or Commonwealth troops riding in a half-track in, for example, Italy in the Second World War. Instead, it is an IDF unit participating in the Yom Hamedina parade in Tel Aviv on 27th July 1948. The Hebrew word "medinah" is literally translated as "state" or "country". "Yom" means "day" and "Ha" is a prefix meaning "the". Therefore, "Yom Hamedina", as in the original photograph caption, literally means "Day of the State", to commemorate the recent establishment of the State of Israel). (*Kluger Zoltan, Israeli Government Press Office*)

These IHC M5 half-tracks are essentially unmodified. They carry troops of the IDF 8th Armoured Brigade on a training exercise somewhere in central Israel on 4th October 1948. Again, the soldiers appear to be well-equipped with British helmets and uniforms. The number "7" in the circle almost looks as though it was written with chalk. (*Kluger Zoltan, Israeli Government Press Office*)

Except for the MG 34s, these troops of the IDF 8th Brigade could just as easily be British. They are involved in the same training exercise in central Israel in October 1948. Note the mix of the familiar Tommy helmet dating back to the First World War, and the later 1944 pattern helmet. The 8th Armoured Brigade consisted of the 82nd Tank Battalion, to which these troops belonged, and the 89th Mechanised Battalion, commanded by Moshe Dayan. On the opposite side of the road is an unmodified Scout Car M3. *(Kluger Zoltan, Israeli Government Press Office)*

Again, this column belongs to the 8th Armoured Brigade, during the same series of manoeuvres. In the original uncropped image, this first company includes seven M5 half-tracks, a single unmodified Scout Car M3 and one Jeep in the lead. Another group follows behind this one. *(Kluger Zoltan, Israeli Government Press Office)*

Half-tracks were active also on the northern front. This group of M5s is part of the 79th Armoured Battalion. The man in the photograph is Ralph Lowenstein, an eighteen-year-old American volunteer, and a driver in that unit. Two companies of the 79th were equipped with unmodified M5s, while the other two companies had converted armoured cars built on the Dodge $\frac{3}{4}$ ton Weapons Carrier. (Ralph Lowenstein)

Ralph Lowenstein now resides in Virginia and has written articles on his experiences with the young IDF. Here, he is pictured standing next to the vehicle that he drove. *(Ralph Lowenstein)*

The half-tracks assigned to the two mechanised infantry companies were unmodified M5s. Another company, or possibly a support platoon, was equipped with "heavy machine guns". The man in the photograph is Mort Levinson, another eighteen-year-old American volunteer, originally from Boston. He was in the infantry squad transported by Ralph Lowenstein. Levinson and Lowenstein shared the distinction of being the youngest American "Machalniks" serving in the IDF at the time. They remain close friends to this day. The vehicles were driven with the armoured windscreen raised, even with the dangers of combat, due to the restricted visibility.
(Ralph Lowenstein)

For some reason, rear views of the IHC half-tracks are rare. The rounded rear corners and Southern Command markings are evident on this M5 on a desert road in the Negev. In the original image, the vehicle tactical number "321", along with two slashes, is visible on the side plate and rear door, identifying the 82nd Tank Battalion, part of the 8th Armoured Brigade.
(David Eldan, Israeli Government Press Office)

This vehicle was built as an IHC M14 or M17 Machine Gun Motor Carriage. Due to the rounded corners, the folding armour at the rear is inset a little. To allow the guns to clear when depressed, the four-gun M16 and M17 had a cutout in the rear plate. The M16 had similar cutouts in the side plates, while it appears as though the M17 did not. The two-gun M13 had straight rear plates, whilst the two-gun M14 was seen with either style. All M17s went to the Soviet Union where they were used as intended. However, the British – who received most of the M14s – converted them to personnel carriers. Since most of these early IDF vehicles were acquired in the United Kingdom and Western Europe, it is very likely that this half-track is one of the converted M14s. It is October 1948 and this vehicle is part of a column advancing toward Beersheba. *(David Eldan, Israeli Government Press Office)*

This very heterogeneous unit, also part of the 82nd Tank Battalion, is at rest near Beersheba. The half-tracks in the foreground have tactical numbers beginning with "2", probably indicating the 2nd Company, versus the third company vehicles in the previous photographs. Along the row of buildings, there are a number of different vehicles visible in the original print, beginning with two converted Scout Cars, an unmodified Otter, two more turreted Scout Cars, a Marmon-Herrington Mark IVF, two turreted Scout Cars and a sandwich truck. *(IDF Spokesman)*

These two M5s have been modified somewhat, with the armoured windscreen cut in half. The co-driver side may now be fixed, and it has a firing slit. They are not yet fitted with a machine gun mount. The scene is in the Negev Desert during the battle for Beersheba on 21st October 1948. *(Hugo Mendelson, Israeli Government Press Office)*

The lead vehicle in the previous photograph is seen here advancing into Beersheba. Barely visible on the side plates in both photographs is a faint and crudely drawn (possibly in chalk) three arrow insignia of Southern Command. *(Hugo Mendelson, Israeli Government Press Office)*

These are the same two vehicles again. Given the rather exposed location of the photographer, plus the fact that the mounted personnel appear to be aiming directly at him, these last two photographs are probably posed. Note that one M5 is equipped with a winch, while the other has a roller. *(Hugo Mendelson, Israeli Government Press Office)*

This vehicle is undergoing some major engine work at a workshop in Sarafand in early December 1948. The entire engine block has been removed, and the large radiator is sitting on the ground. *(Israeli Government Press Office)*

Three half-tracks, a converted armoured car and a lorry are in various stages of repair at the same facility. The locations for the markings are unusual, as are the Hebrew letters in place of the serial number on the third vehicle. *(Israeli Government Press Office)*

These mechanics are adjusting the tracks on what appears to be a M14 MGMC, less the gun turret. As such, it is probably one of the ex-British Army vehicles acquired in the United Kingdom. The officer is the same person overseeing the engine work in the earlier photograph. In front are a M5 and a converted M3 Scout Car. *(Israeli Government Press Office)*

Behind the girl, note that there is glass visible through the vision slit on the co-driver's side, whilst the driver has a visor with bulletproof glass. The serial number was applied neatly with a stencil, but the black rectangle was painted free hand. Also note the girl soldier in front of the half-track; she has rested her rifle on the mudguard whilst she uses a civilian-issue hairbrush. *(Israeli Government Press Office)*

This column of half-tracks from the 82nd Tank Battalion is advancing along a road in the Negev on its way to Egypt during Operation Horev in December 1948. Markings include the vehicle identification number, the three arrows of Southern Command, two slashes and the number "313". These M5s probably came from Britain. Wartime photographs of British half-tracks show the same non-standard lights. Note that on many of these vehicles the jerrican racks have been removed. *(Israeli Government Press Office)*

Troops mount unmodified M5 half-tracks in preparation for the battle for Abu Agela. Markings are not visible, but the unit is very likely the 82nd Tank Battalion. *(Israeli Government Press Office)*

The crew of this M5 checks out fuel captured from the Egyptians at Abu Agela, during Operation Horev. They wear a mix of uniforms, including splinter camouflage, while the web gear seems to be American or French in origin. The machine gun is covered, so apparently the fighting is over. *(Israeli Government Press Office)*

The M5 was not equipped with a skate rail for the machine guns – at least, not as standard equipment. This may be a M3 Scout Car, but the rail is not like the one usually installed in that vehicle either. Either way, this is a command vehicle of some sort, as indicated by the multiple antennae. *(Israeli Government Press Office)*

In contrast with some of the well-equipped troops in a few of the previous photographs, this group presents a very motley appearance. No two people are dressed the same, and there is a mix of weapons and web gear as well. There is also one woman in the foreground group, and possibly another in front of the GMC truck. Note the Hebrew lettering at an angle on the M5 to the right. Special note: the weapon in the rear of this half-track is a flame-thrower. The location is Chalutza in the Negev, 15th December 1948 during Operation Horev. *(Israeli Government Press Office)*

One of these homegrown flame-throwers is shown here being tested at the Ramat Hasharon engineer school. Sources say at least two half-tracks carried the weapon. The vehicle in the previous photograph is one of them, which makes it a rarity. *(Israeli Government Press Office)*

This nearly complete flame-thrower and fuel tank is displayed at The Collection Houses in Tel-Aviv-Jaffa (Jafo, as pronounced in Hebrew). The propellant was housed in the rear of the weapon; the lever below controlled the flow, while the trigger on the side released the fuel. *(Josh Weingarten)*

This is the left side of the unit. *(Josh Weingarten)*

Judging by the relative height of the unit and its position in the vehicle, the tank was mounted over the well between the tracks. Most likely, the side flanges seen here were bolted to a frame attached to the top of the track covers. The presence of the circular plate on the bottom suggests that perhaps there was a second fuel tank beneath. *(Josh Weingarten)*

Elevation and traverse was via a ball mount, upon which this weapon is slightly askew. Note the fuel gauge between the two cylinders, as well as the perforations in the nozzle. The black cylinders on the wall are unrelated. *(Josh Weingarten)*

These troops are taking part in Operation Horev in December 1948. The half-track crew appears to be in a relaxed mood, while the Jeep driver looks poised to move out. The location is near Abu Agela. *(Israeli Government Press Office)*

IDF troops advance into Egypt during the battle for Abu Agela. The wide variety of transport utilised by the IDF, including buses, is evident. The half-tracks are normal M5s. The small white marking is the three arrow emblem of Southern Command. *(Israeli Government Press Office)*

Even in victory, the cost to the Israeli forces was considerable: this M5 of the 8th Armoured Brigade has literally been blown apart. The resulting fire incinerated the rubber tyre and the rubber on the tracks. *(Ralph Lowenstein)*

The desert can be quite cold in the winter, as evidenced by the overcoats seen here, and also in many of the photographs of the Second World War North African campaigns. This column of mixed vehicles is advancing during Operation Horev on 15th December 1948. In the foreground is an almost standard M5 IHC half-track. The only modifications appear to be a bullet-proof glass visor replacing the normal sliding panel on the driver's side, and an internal linkage or bracket for supporting the open armoured windscreen. The normal supports are lying flat on the bonnet (hood for those of us who live in the Colonies). It is also missing the front roller assembly. The three-arrows marking is the insignia of Southern Command. Behind this M5 are four more half-tracks, an American 2½ ton GMC truck, a bus troop transport and a Bedford QL 3-ton lorry. *(Israeli Government Press Office)*

This IHC M5 passes a soldier checking out the sign at the El Arish crossroads in the Sinai Desert. The vehicle is similar to the ones shown previously in Beersheba. The right side of the armoured windscreen is probably fixed in place. *(Israeli Government Press Office)*

This M5 has paused along the road while advancing through the Negev in December 1948. The burned-out CMP lorry in the foreground could be either Egyptian or Israeli. *(Israeli Government Press Office)*

Although this photograph is a little fuzzy and dark, it shows the character of the Sinai Desert at dusk. This IDF column is advancing during the battle for Abu Agela. They are unmodified International-Harvester M5s, with crews that are dressed for the cold of December in the desert. Combat is not imminent, since the first vehicle's machine gun is still covered. Note that the second half-track has its front armour slats closed, giving it the appearance of the more modern diesel versions. *(Israeli Government Press Office)*

This column is passing vehicles wrecked during earlier combat. There are several photographs in this series, all of which show damaged or destroyed lorries, evidence perhaps that Egyptian aircraft strafed an IDF supply column. The machine guns are covered here, indicating at least a lull, if not the end of combat. *(Israeli Government Press Office)*

This group of vehicles has turned in the direction of fighting in the distance. The battle for Abu Agela may be raging at this point. In the original print, although fuzzy, there are at least three radio antennae on the half-track. *(Israeli Government Press Office)*

The crew of this half-track is preparing for bivouac for the evening. Given the lack of coats, it is too warm to be morning. One man cleans his weapon, as the others cover the vehicle with a net. Note the tripod for a heavy machine gun of some sort. *(Israeli Government Press Office)*

This M5 carries a crew dressed in British uniforms. Note that the soldier on the left, inside the vehicle, is armed with a Boys anti-tank rifle, while the one on the right has a MG 34 – an interesting contrast. *(Israeli Government Press Office)*

This photograph was taken some time after the end of a battle, probably in the Negev or Sinai. Note the mix of uniform items, including British helmets and American leggings. The half-track may have struck an anti-personnel mine or otherwise received light damage to the engine bay, tyres and mudguards. Note that the armoured visor on the driver's door, which is on the inside, identifying the vehicle as an International Harvester M5. *(IDF Archives, Ministry of Defence)*

Half-tracks, General Use, 1948 to 1959

Not much is visible in this photograph, taken on Army Day in July 1949, except it is useful for markings. Barely visible in the original image are three B-17 bombers of the Israeli Air Force flying over the festivities. These Flying Fortresses were acquired in the United States, and smuggled out of the country in June 1948. Reconditioned in Czechoslovakia, they were flown to Israel in July, bombing Cairo and other targets on the way. *(David Eldan, Israeli Government Press Office)*

This vehicle's crew appears to be ready for a parade. They have unit patches on their arms, which would seem to indicate that the War of Independence is long over, and the IDF has become a professional organisation. Note also the colourful unit insignia of the famous 7th Armoured Brigade, which now included the 79th Armoured Battalion. *(Ralph Lowenstein)*

These 7th Armoured Brigade M5s are, indeed, participating in a post-war parade: Liberation Day in April 1949, in Haifa. Note the prominent insignia of this unit. The crew appears to be equipped with the British airborne helmet. *(Teddy Brauner, Israeli Government Press Office)*

These vehicles are part of exercises in the early 1950s. Little has changed since the war, but the identification number sequence, as is visible in the original photograph, is inappropriate for that time period. The half-track is a normal M5, without a front-mounted machine gun, while the Jeep appears to be a CJ2A.

Half-tracks, General Use, 1948 to 1959

This M5A1 or M9A1 is participating in exercises in September 1951. These two vehicles are indistinguishable from the outside. As manufactured, the M5A1 was the counterpart of the M3A1 troop carrier, and the M9A1 was similar to the Half-track Car M2A1. The main differences between the M9A1 and M2/M2A1 are that the M9A1 does not have external access doors for the side stowage bins, and it does have a rear door. This half-track is fitted out as a command vehicle, with additional radios. Instead of the normal M2HB .50 calibre machine gun, it is armed with a Besa – like many of the Shermans of the period. Note, also, that it has two bulletproof visors for the driver and co-driver. Visible in the original print is an unusual serial number, "82127" followed by four Hebrew letters. The marking on the bonnet is a blue Shield of David on a white disc. Also visible in the photograph are a couple of Jeeps and a $\frac{3}{4}$ ton Weapons Carrier. *(Eldan David, Israeli Government Press Office)*

These modified M5s are participating in the Independence Day (Yom Ha Atzmaut) parade in Tel Aviv on 30th April 1952. The first two, at least, have a ball-mounted MG 34 for the co-driver, along with bulletproof visors for both. The right-side shield appears to be fixed in its lowered position. IDF vehicles at this time were painted olive drab. The air-recognition marking is again a blue Magen David (Shield of David) on a white disc. The emblem on the mudguard is the insignia of the 7th Armoured Brigade. This unit, as the 7th Mechanised Brigade, was Israel's first armoured unit, being formed on 9th May 1948 – a full week before independence was declared. *(Israeli Government Press Office)*

These troops are involved in manoeuvres in the Negev in September 1954. The M5 in the foreground is fitted with the early form of co-driver machine gun mount, but the usual MG 34 is missing. The IDF's primary source of weapons at this stage was Czechoslovakia, which explains the MG 34 and 98K rifles. The uniforms appear to be British in origin. *(Israeli Government Press Office)*

This is a rear view of the same M5 as in the previous photograph. *(Israeli Government Press Office)*

Without seeing the interior, it is impossible to tell whether this is an M5A1 or a M9A1. With the extra antennae, this appears to be a command vehicle. The location is once again in the Negev Desert, this time in December 1955. *(Israeli Government Press Office)*

The years between wars were filled with skirmishes and retaliatory responses to attacks by Arab *fedayeen*. This group is returning from just such a raid, sometime during 1955. The lead vehicle is a M5A1 or M9A1, mounting several Besa series machine guns. The second half-track is fitted with the early style of co-driver machine gun mount, with an MG 34. *(IDF Archives, Ministry of Defence)*

The next major campaign for the young Israel Defence Force was Operation Kadesh, also known as the Sinai Campaign, in late 1956. The Israelis joined in a joint effort with the French and British to take control of the Suez Canal, after it was nationalised by Egypt's President Nasser. The Israeli effort consisted of a rapid armoured advance across the Sinai Desert. This column of half-tracks is racing along toward the Canal. The sign is Arabic for "Go Slow". Even though the crew appears to be relaxed, they are prepared for combat, as indicated by the closed windscreen armour. *(Israeli Government Press Office)*

A column stops to check their location on a map. The half-tracks are unmodified M5s, armed with pedestal-mounted Besa machine guns. The troops are also carrying MG 34s. At this stage, IDF soldiers wear a mix of uniforms, including British and American helmets. *(IDF Archives, Ministry of Defence)*

This armoured column includes half-tracks, AMX-13 light tanks and Jeeps. The "X" marking is commonly seen on all types of vehicles during the 1956 campaign, including Sherman tanks. Note also the Magen David (Shield of David) on the half-track's bonnet. *(IDF Archives, Ministry of Defence)*

Israeli troops enter a building, in what appears to be a quiet sector, given their casual appearance. These M5s carry pedestal-mounted MG 34s, instead of the Besa machine guns in the previous photographs. The air recognition Magen David is dust covered, but still discernable. *(IDF Archives, Ministry of Defence)*

Although the IDF had begun receiving M2/M3 type half-tracks from several sources including France, these vehicles are M5s. This towed artillery unit, equipped with 25-pounders, is returning to Israel on 5th December 1956. Note how clearly the blue Magen David on the white disc stands out against the olive drab background. *(Israeli Government Press Office)*

The same unit is now passing the northern checkpoint at El Arish later in the day. The blue Magen David is not very clear and may have been replaced on this vehicle by a blue "X" on the white disc. The serial number on the first vehicle begins with "7". *(Israeli Government Press Office)*

Another M5 approaches a number of wrecked Egyptian vehicles in the Sinai Peninsula on 3rd November 1956. The centre vehicle is a Scammell tractor. Note the Arabic writing on the licence plate of the lorry on the right. No markings are visible on the half-track, but it likely has a Magen David on the bonnet and a serial number on the rear bumper. *(Israeli Government Press Office)*

This is Aluf (General) Chaim Laskov (top left) with his staff officers at Rafa, November 1956. This half-track has extra antennae, but is otherwise unadorned. Compare this to later command vehicles. Note that the uniforms are distinctly British in appearance. *(Israeli Government Press Office)*

This column is on the road from El Arish to Rafa on 15th January 1957. The IDF refers to vehicles with the ring mount, in this case either a M5A1 or M9A1, as the M3 Mark B. Earlier production vehicles with the pedestal mount are designated M3 Mark A. Here, the second vehicle in line is a Mark B, followed by more Mark A's. *(Israeli Government Press Office)*

This column of vehicles is prepared to leave El Arish on the same day. The appearance of the vehicles and troops has changed very little from eight years earlier. The half-tracks are basic IHC Mk 5s. *(Israeli Government Press Office)*

The same column of half-tracks is halted at the border crossing between Rafa and El Arish later that day. Note the souvenir Egyptian licence plate on the front of this M3 Mark B, which is just visible on the second vehicle in the previous photograph. Note also the bazooka in the rear, as well as the chalked markings on the front of the ring mount. *(Israeli Government Press Office)*

Led by an unmodified M5, this column of trucks is also returning to Israel at the end of the campaign. The muzzle of an MG 34 is just visible behind the one soldier. *(IDF Archives, Ministry of Defence)*

Colonel Meir, the officer in charge of the final IDF withdrawal from the Sinai after the armistice, says farewell to his United Nations counterpart on 6th March 1957. The vehicle is either an M5A1 or a M9A1 Mark B. Given its passenger, it is probably a command vehicle. Although no markings are visible, it will have the standard identification number: white numbers on a black rectangle, over an olive drab finish. *(Israeli Government Press Office)*

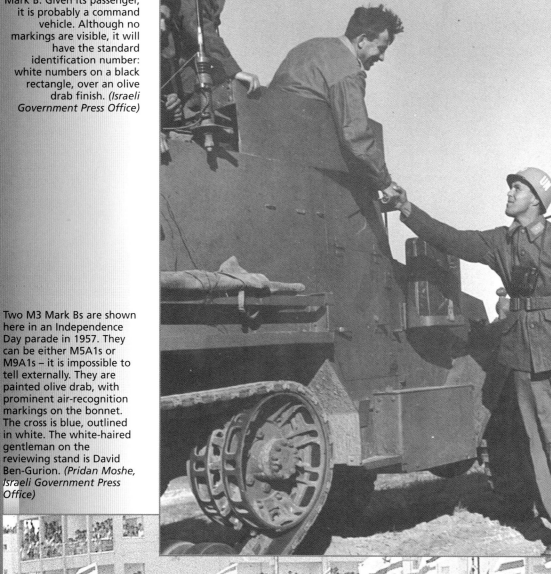

Two M3 Mark Bs are shown here in an Independence Day parade in 1957. They can be either M5A1s or M9A1s – it is impossible to tell externally. They are painted olive drab, with prominent air-recognition markings on the bonnet. The cross is blue, outlined in white. The white-haired gentleman on the reviewing stand is David Ben-Gurion. *(Pridan Moshe, Israeli Government Press Office)*

Chapter Five Half-tracks, Modified

To make up, in part, for a relative lack of firepower pending the acquisition of tanks, the IDF improvised self-propelled guns using some of the first batch of half-tracks. Although this particular unidentified gun appears to be bent, it is not: the cover is simply larger than the diameter of the barrel. The shield is clearly makeshift, while the gun itself appears to be about the size of a 37 mm. It was not uncommon for these early vehicles to lack both the winch and roller. The crew is enjoying a game of cards somewhere along the Israel/Lebanon border in November 1948. *(Israeli Government Press Office)*

This IHC M5 from the 82nd Tank Battalion has a more normal appearance, with a 6-pounder in a configuration similar to the US Gun Motor Carriage M3. Judging by the bulkiness of the cover over the end of the barrel, this is the later Mark IV version with a longer barrel and a muzzle brake. The driver's compartment has a partial roof and a right-side ball-mounted machine gun. It leads a long column of vehicles, including a Scammell tractor, on a road in the Negev Desert, during Operation Horev in December 1948. Markings include the three arrows of southern Command, and the number 3282 on the side of the bonnet. Based on photographs of other vehicles in this unit, there is also, likely, a three-digit number (perhaps 332), and two forward slashes, on the hull side. Note that the headlamp is non-standard. The upper armoured radiator flap is closed while the others are open. *(Israeli Government Press Office)*

This photograph is from the private collection of Hertz Hershberg, the commander of this unit; he is the gentleman in the middle, with the spectacles. According to Hershberg, there were only three of these conversions done, so all of them are covered here in this book. This is the only one of the three that does not have the side mine racks, so it is readily recognisable. *(Hertz Hershberg)*

This is another 6-pounder half-track from the 82nd Tank Battalion, also listed as 82nd Armoured Battalion, part of the 8th Brigade. It carries a slightly different style of markings, although the three-arrow Southern Command sign is present - albeit in a different location. The other markings, barely visible, appear to be shipping stencils or something similar. There is also what appears to be a vehicle serial number, "10633", crudely painted just forward of the arrows. There is also no front ball-mounted machine gun, and the radio is on the opposite side from that in the previous vehicle. Given the sleeveless undershirts in evidence, the time must be summer. *(Ralph Lowenstein)*

This is "10633" again, still during relatively mild weather. The data stencils are from immediately after the Second World War. The one above the vehicle number is the size and weight in cubic feet and pounds. The one beneath the arrows is largely illegible, but after analysis, the centre label reads: TO. C.O. , LETTERKENNY ARMY DEPOT; CAR (*illegible*); CHAMBERSBURG, PA.; G-C-541 (*illegible*).
The rear marking reads: ANTI- FREEZE INSTALLED; GAS TANK DRAINED; PREPARED FOR LONG TERM (*covered up*); NOV. 7 1945; FROM. U.S. ARMY SECTION.; L.O.P.D. MONTREAL QUEBEC. Letterkenny Army Depot was used for storage of returned vehicles and ordnance after the war. There is also a Canadian depot in Longueuile in the province of Quebec, so perhaps this vehicle was originally intended for return to the United States after its service with the Canadian Army. *(Hertz Hershberg)*

Hershberg is reviewing a map with his men. The vehicles include the first half-track shown, identified by its front winch and markings, on the right. The vehicle on the left is the third converted half-track. This is confirmed by the presence of a front ball-mounted machine gun, missing on the second vehicle shown, "10633". *(Hertz Hershberg)*

This is also "10633". It has been repainted, leaving the number with a slight overspray. This was evidently done after the stationary shield was added in front of the gun. The weather is better, but still chilly, so it is probably spring 1949. There is a truce in effect, and there is time for some levity. It may be an optical illusion, but the new colour seems to be a little lighter than the original. Given the intact stencilling, this earlier colour was probably British or bronze green. *(Hertz Hershberg)*

Although it is difficult to be sure, this is probably "10633" again. (The shield seems to be different from that on vehicle number three). This is a happy group, so it is most likely well after the fighting is over. *(Hertz Hershberg)*

This is a third example of a 6-pounder equipped half-track, before the application of the white markings shown in the next photograph. This vehicle has the ball-mounted machine gun, as in the first example, plus a fixed gun shield in front of the standard 6-pounder shield.

While there are differences between them, all three of these conversions have the partial roof over the front compartment. The shape of the fixed shield is more evident here. There is even a view slit in the shield, to correspond with the gunner's view port on the 6-pounder shield. Note that these half-track crews wear the Soviet-style tanker's helmet. These are actually brown copies made in Czechoslovakia. The MG 34 in the ball-mount is also from Czechoslovakia. *(Ralph Lowenstein)*

This M5 has a partial roof covering approximately seventy-five per cent of the rear compartment, with an open-top turret mounting a 20 mm gun. The drivers' area is also covered, with the ball-mounted MG 34 on the right side. Once again, there is a bulletproof visor for the driver. This unit is participating in Operation Horev, 12th December 1948. *(Israeli Government Press Office)*

This is the same vehicle, with the turret traversed. Given the way that the stowage is tied on, there are either tie-downs on the roof, or there is a framework supporting the turret. This could mean that the roof does not completely cover the area, but that does not seem practical. The radio antennae is at the rear. Note the mount for a MG 34 on the left rear corner. Just forward of this is the rack for the pioneer tools, which looks like it is welded to the side. *(Israeli Government Press Office)*

This view shows the driver's visor and the ball-mounted MG 34 to good advantage. Note also the linkage for raising and lowering the armoured windscreen. This is not an original fitting to IHC half-tracks. The mix of uniform items is interesting, especially the footwear. *(Israeli Government Press Office)*

This rear view of the same vehicle has several points of interest. The spare tyre is mounted on the rear door. The antennae is British, and there is a second MG 34 pintle mount on the right rear corner. The faces of the crew prove that this is the same vehicle as in the preceding photographs. The soldier with the moustache is the driver, while the one with the smile is the soldier not waving in the earlier shot. This also illustrates that the troop compartment was open behind the turret. *(Israeli Government Press Office)*

This photograph confirms that this type of vehicle was probably produced in numbers to a common design. There are subtle differences in the turret, and there is no rack for the spare tyre on the rear door. In this case, the antennae is not mounted at the rear, and, for some reason, has been stuck into a tie-down on the right side. Note that there is a door from the driver's compartment into the fighting compartment. Since the turret is forward, the fuel tanks have probably been relocated to the rear. This half-track is refuelling on 15th December 1948. *(Israeli Government Press Office)*

Not all IDF light support weapons were MG 34s. This half-track crewman is using a Bren gun. The standard mount for the MG 34 is, however, still available, but it is in use as a helmet rack in this case. *(Israeli Government Press Office)*

In another posed shot by the same crew, a Bren gun is shown in the swivel mount. Note that the magazine is not fitted this time. The turret is traversed to the rear, with the gun visible below the Bren. *(Israeli Government Press Office)*

This group of Southern Command soldiers is in formation near Chalutza in the Negev, December 1948. The vehicle is one of the turreted conversions, but the turret itself is covered with a tarpaulin. The outline is discernable at the rear, while the 20 mm gun protrudes from the front. After analysing the following photographs, this may be the vehicle with the larger turret. *(Israeli Government Press Office)*

This is a towed version of the 20 mm gun anti-tank gun that was subsequently mounted in these half-tracks. The original caption, from the same time frame as the previous photographs, states that it is a captured Egyptian weapon. In this case, that may very well be true. However, the IDF must have acquired the gun in quantity previously, because the half-track conversions are quite elaborate, and would have taken quite a long time to complete. *(Israeli Government Press Office)*

IDF armoured units advance toward Abu Agela in the Egyptian desert during Operation Horev on 15th December 1948. The vehicle on the left is a modified M3 Scout Car. The half-track appears to be similar to the one in the previous photograph. However, the roof covers only the driver area, and the turret is larger. Other photographs in the same series show the weapon to be the same type of 20 mm gun. *(Israeli Government Press Office)*

Even at a distance, the large size of this turret is very evident. At first glance, it appears to be fixed, making this conversion more like an assault gun. However, the following photograph dispels this idea. The group of vehicles includes at least three converted M3 Scout Cars and a captured lorry, still bearing Egyptian markings. *(Israeli Government Press Office)*

From a distance, it is difficult to see the identification number, but this is the same vehicle as in the previous two photographs: 2512-Y. The turret is traversed to the left rear. In the original photograph, there is a series of bullet ricochets to the right, indicating that they are under fire. This is also supported by the fact that no crewmen are visible. *(Israeli Government Press Office)*

The third vehicle also appears to be the same half-track as in the previous series of photographs. In front is a Jeep, then an unmodified M5 half-track. The M5 does not have a co-driver machine gun, while the turreted version does. Although of poor quality, this enlargement of a portion of a wartime photograph is used here because images of the early modified vehicles are quite rare. *(Israeli Government Press Office)*

Although taken near sunset and rather dark, this photograph confirms that the same 20 mm gun was carried in this version. Note also that there is what looks to be a periscope mounted above the co-driver's machine gun. The vehicle number is the same as the one in the first photograph of this conversion. *(Israeli Government Press Office)*

This is a much more elaborate conversion, pictured after the War of Independence. Some of the half-tracks obtained from scrap dealers had been de-militarised by removing much or all of the rear armour. This vehicle has been rebuilt almost completely from the firewall back. The turret is from an ex-British Daimler armoured car, while the one over the co-driver position is one of the standardised indigenous designs. It even has side hatches. At this time, Czechoslovakia was a primary arms supplier, so Besa and MG 34 machine guns are common. *(IDF Spokesman)*

As shown with the previously discussed sandwich trucks and armoured cars, the IDF developed a number of makeshift armoured vehicles to compensate for the lack of the real thing. This self-propelled light anti-aircraft unit is passing the reviewing stand during the Army Day parade in Tel Aviv on 17th July 1949. The conversions were done on American $2\frac{1}{2}$ ton GMC lorries. At least three are visible in the photograph, so this is probably a standard vehicle. *(Eldan David, Israeli Government Press Office)*

About the Author

Born in January 1949, the author grew up near Baltimore, Maryland, in the United States. A business credit manager by profession, his hobby interests include armour modelling and researching Sherman tanks and the Israeli Defence Forces. He is a regular visitor to various Internet armour discussion forums, and he has presented seminars on armour subjects at model shows in the US. He has two adult children, Bryan and Heather (Eyler) and one granddaughter, Julia Eyler. He presently lives in Maryland and is engaged to Connie Baker.

The author (far right) is shown here on a visit to Israel in 2005. From the left: Joshua Weingarten, a good friend and contributor, and Hirsh Hertzberg, an Israeli veteran featured in this book.

The following people contributed photographs used in this book:
Joshua Weingarten, USA
David Levy, Israel
Erin Kaufman, Israel
Hirsh Hertzberg, Israel
Mark Hazzard, UK
Ralph Lowenstein, USA
Frans van Starkenburg, Netherlands
Adib Yazbeck, Lebanon
Jan-Willem de Boer, Netherlands
John Myszka, Australia
Pierre-Olivier Baun, France
Emmanuel Bennayoun, France
Ian Sadler, UK
Bill Whitley, USA
Vasko Barbic, UK
Illan Levy